For King and

GW01466482

For King and Country

Four Brothers, Four Crosses

A NEW ZEALAND STORY

Jock Vennell

Wily Publications Ltd

Published by Wily Publications Ltd
302 Lake Terrace Road, Christchurch 8061
New Zealand
email: jjhaworth@xtra.co.nz
www.wily.co.nz
First published 2019

ISBN 978-1-927167-39-7

Front cover background image:
Messines battlefield, Belgium, during World War I, with shells bursting in
the distance. Royal New Zealand Returned and Services' Association :New
Zealand official negatives, World War 1914-1918.
Ref: 1/2-012776-G. Alexander Turnbull Library, Wellington, New Zealand. /records/22802881

Front cover family image:
For King and country. Victor (seated in front) with his three brothers before
the war, left to right, Herbert, Julian and Reginald.
Christophers family archive

Cover, book design and page layout:
Quentin Wilson, Christchurch
wilson.quentin@gmail.com

Printed in Taipei, Taiwan (ROC) by
CHOICE Printing Inc.

CONTENTS

PROLOGUE

"Strange friend," I said, "here is no cause to mourn."
"None," said the other, "save the undone years,
The hopelessness. Whatever hope is yours,
Was my life also; I went hunting wild
After the wildest beauty in the world,
Which lies not calm in eyes, or braided hair,
But mocks the steady running of the hour,
And if it grieves, grieves richlier than here.
For by my glee might many men have laughed,
And of my weeping something had been left,
Which must die now. I mean the truth untold,
The pity of war, the pity war distilled.

Strange Meeting by World War I soldier-poet Wilfred Owen.

Two soldiers meet in an imagined Hell, the first having killed the second in battle and now mourns the tragic waste of war. Owen himself would not live to see its end in 1918.

INTRODUCTION

World War I had a profound and lasting impact on New Zealand's culture and society, wrote military historian Ian McGibbon in 2016. The first and greatest was the loss of the best of a generation—18,500 dead from disease or battle wounds, and countless others so physically and mentally damaged that they could play no useful part in post-war society. War imposed a huge economic cost on a nation still in the early stages of development, and caused major disruption to nationally important industries and social services. There was the loss of basic freedoms, if only temporarily, that came with wartime censorship and conscription.

On the positive side, the war encouraged women in their thousands onto farms and into factories and offices to take the place of men serving overseas. Other impacts were less tangible, among them the war novels, memoirs and histories that enriched our literature for the remainder of the 20th century, and particularly the boost World War I gave to our identity as New Zealanders. The years between the Anzac landings at Gallipoli and the black swamp of Passchendaele, wrote soldier and post-war pacifist Ormond Burton, were a critical point in the development of a sense of national identity—a time in which New Zealand, in the crucible of war, became aware of itself as a nation.

Through the lives and deaths of four brothers from a small New Zealand town this book attempts to throw light on the impact of World War I on a developing colonial society and its true cost in the destruction of so many of its coming generation. Young New Zealanders went to war, Ormond Burton wrote, "ignorant of its causes, and innocent of its meaning. No alternative was suggested by the politicians, or the Press, or the parsons. To crowds of ordinary boys there seemed to be no other possible or decent thing to do but to go out and fight."[1]

Four years on, their country would count the cost. As a former Chancellor of Auckland University, Sir Douglas Robb, put it: "In all walks of life many of those who would have been the leaders were missing. The ineptitudes of the decades between the two wars, both in Europe and New Zealand, may in large measure be due to this. Not only these men, but those who would have been their children are missing, and we have had to do our best without them."[2] Among the major sufferers were our women who had to deal not only with the loss of husbands, brothers, lovers and friends, but also with the thousands of physically and mentally damaged men who survived to return home.

"It seems to be a New Zealand tradition to fight in foreign wars not of our making," observed historian Christopher Pugsley in his groundbreaking book on the Gallipoli campaign.[3] But if this country had no part in making this war, it had a large interest in seeing it finished with Germany's complete defeat. The four Christophers brothers, like most of their generation, went willingly to war for that. "For the first and only time," wrote Pugsley again, "they had identified with a cause bigger than themselves and had known what it meant to be a man."

1

IN THE BEGINNING

In August 1862, a 19-year-old youth by the name of Anthony Christophers stepped ashore at Bluff Harbour after a stormy five-day voyage
across the Tasman. It was a bare 40 years after Southland's first European
immigrants had settled on its coast, many of them sealers and whalers from
the penal colonies of Australia. In the taverns and streets of the new town of
Invercargill rough Australian gold diggers rubbed shoulders with Scottish
and Irish settlers, by now making up 60 per cent of Southland's population.

In 1844, Frederick Tuckett had come south, searching for a site for a
settlement of members of the Free Church of Scotland. The area around
Bluff and Riverton, he noted in disgust, was "a mere bog utterly unfit for
human habitation."[4] Six years later, Captain John Stokes took his survey
ship *Acheron* into Bluff Harbour. After exploring the Oreti and Aparima
rivers by whaleboat, he returned convinced that he had found an area of
potentially rich farmland eminently suitable for European settlement.

In 1853, the Government bought the massive Murihiku Block from its
tribal owners, consisting of all land south-west of a line from the Nuggets to
just north of Milford Sound—some 10,500 square miles of territory in all.
Organised settlement in Southland now began. Large blocks of land were
purchased from the Crown, flocks of sheep shipped across the Tasman and
driven through bogs, swamps and forest to their runs deep in the interior.

The pioneers and their families came in from Otago in the north or

The Christophers family ten years before the war. Left to right at rear are sons Victor, Julian and Herbert. In front are father Anthony, youngest son Quintin, mother Juliet and oldest son Reginald.

Christophers family archive

by sea to Riverton or Bluff and then inland by small boat up the great Southland rivers. They arrived on foot, horseback or bullock wagon, a journey that could take up to six weeks if conditions were bad. The sea journey between Dunedin and Invercargill—in the early days the only route possible between the two towns—might take two weeks or more if the winds were unfavourable and the seas stormy.

The land the newcomers now occupied was largely covered in forest or dense growths of flax, tussock and matagouri, all of which had to be cleared, mainly by fire. Their accommodation was basic, often a one or two-roomed thatched cottage built of slabs of rough-sawn timber with a hard-dirt floor. The food, in the early days at least, was plain to the point of malnutrition—sheep meat, bread, potatoes, sugar and black tea. Life for most was rough and raw.

In 1861 came the great Otago goldrush. "Farmers forsook their farms, shopkeepers their shops, and artisans their benches," wrote a local historian.[5] As the news spread wider afield, thousands of miners from the Victorian goldfields poured across the Tasman to search for gold in Southland's main rivers—the Waiau, Aparima, Oreti and Mataura.

A year later, Anthony Christophers arrived from Castlemaine in the Australian state of Victoria, not to dig or pan for gold, but to take up a position with the Bank of New South Wales. Over the next 30 years he managed in succession the bank's Clyde, Lawrence and Timaru branches before taking over its Invercargill branch in 1891. At this time the bank was playing a key role in supplying capital and banking services to the settlers and new businesses springing up in Invercargill and in small towns throughout the province.

In 1877, Anthony married Juliet Mary Gillon and together they brought up their five sons—Reginald, Julian, Victor, Herbert, and Quintin—all born between 1882 and 1896. The Christophers boys, like many of their colonial contemporaries, were the grandsons of immigrants originally from the British Isles who had settled first in Australia. Their earliest known ancestors were natives of the county of Devon in England, where in 1804 John Christophers of Ashhurst wed Suzanne Steer of Bovey Tracey. Not unusually for the time John and Suzanne had a large family—18 children, 16 of whom appear to have survived infancy. Among the survivors was Henry, born at Dartmouth in 1806. According to family sources, he joined the Royal Navy as a young man, rising steadily through the ranks to reach the rank of captain.

In his twenties, Henry emigrated to Brazil where he spent the next 25 years in unspecified business activities, including 19 months as acting British consul in the city of Pernambuco. It was there in 1840 that he married Clara Luiza Marques da Costa Soares, granddaughter of an "eminent merchant" of that city and of mixed Portuguese and English extraction. Henry's business enterprises may have fallen on hard times for in 1853, he, Clara and their seven children sailed from Brazil for Australia, to better, as Henry put it, "my poor fortunes" and provide for their large and growing family. Meanwhile, he had approached the British Foreign Office seeking its help in securing a post in some area of colonial government on their arrival in Australia.

The month-long voyage to Melbourne on the emigrant ship *Digby* was memorable but for all the wrong reasons. Henry fell out early with the captain and his first mate over the latter's drunken and abusive behaviour towards himself and other passengers. After landfall in Melbourne's Port Phillip Bay, he wrote to his mother: "The voyage altogether (was) one bundle of atrocities, drunkenness, disorder, riots, mutinies, and blackguardism from the captain's berth aft to the windlass... Cursing, swearing, the most awful and lowest imprecations, have prevailed from the captain downward from beginning to end."[6]

The family arrived intact, but there is no record of complaints from the ship's passengers or an inquiry into the events on board as alleged by Henry Christophers, himself a former captain in the Royal Navy. The government post he sought appears not to have eventuated, and he and his family finally settled in the goldfields town of Castlemaine, 120 kilometres north-west of Melbourne. Henry seems to have resisted the lure of gold prospecting for he emerged next as Castlemaine's first town clerk and later as a member of the town council.

The second of Henry and Clara's children was Anthony, born in London in 1843 but raised with his other siblings in Brazil and then Australia. At the age of 14, he joined the Bank of New South Wales and five years later was transferred across the Tasman to Dunedin and what became a long and successful career with the bank.

By the early 1890s, the Christophers family were established members of Invercargill's social elite, regular churchgoers and most likely comfortably off. Described as being "of a most kindly and unassuming nature, just and upright,"[7] Anthony was active in community affairs as president of the Invercargill Club and the Invercargill Football Club, and vice-president of its rowing club. As a Justice of the Peace, he was also a de facto magistrate, charged with hearing a variety of petty offences, including drunkenness, assault and disorderly behaviour.

Anthony and Juliet's five sons all attended Southland Boys' High School where all were prominent sportsmen, excelling in athletics, rugby, rowing, tennis and cricket. At the outbreak of war in 1914, all except Quintin were established in the early stages of their various careers. Victor was a clerk with a stock and station firm in Invercargill, Herbert an engineering draftsman in the North Island town of Ohakune, Julian a manager for another stock and station firm in the east coast town of Wairoa. Reginald was a civil engineer working in California on the Western Pacific Railway and other projects connected with the state's expanding railway networks.

Their lives were comfortable and so far unremarkable, but the catastrophe that would overtake European civilisation in 1914, their country and their family, was about to unfold. By the end of World War I in November 1918, only Quintin, the youngest of Anthony and Juliet's sons, would still be alive. One hundred years on, this is their story.

Victor (Vic) Christophers.

Christophers family archives

2

VICTOR JAMES ("VIC")

Nearly all men have the desire to serve great ends, to match
themselves with circumstances, to dare the risks of great adventures.
Pleasure and security can never finally satisfy. There are always
horizons that must be reached, hills that must be climbed, a fleece
of gold to be snatched even from the dark wood of the War God.
　　　　　　　　 – Soldier and post-war pacifist Ormond Burton

The first of the Christophers brothers to enlist for service overseas was
Victor ("Vic") Christophers, one of four brothers who would serve
at Gallipoli and on the Western Front during World War I. Apart from an
active involvement in the school cadets, there is no evidence that Vic had a
strong interest in things military. Before he had finished secondary school,
however, his country had sent its first soldiers to a foreign conflict—the
South African War of 1899–1902.

Some 6000 mounted riflemen would fight in that war to defend imperial
interests in South Africa. They would perform with distinction in engage-
ments at Slingersfontein, Ottoshoop, Wildfontein, and Langverwacht. They
would return home with a reputation as perhaps the best mounted troops in
the British army in South Africa—brave, physically tough and resourceful,
true sons, in the eyes of many, of the nation's hardy pioneers.

Much repeated was the comment in the official *Times* history that the
New Zealanders were "by general consent regarded as, on an average, the
best mounted troops in South Africa." British Commander in Chief Lord
Wolseley had rated them "better than any troops I know of in Europe,"
including his own.[8] By the turn of the century, observed social historian
Steven Loveridge, New Zealand men were reputed to possess mental and
physical qualities that made them natural soldiers.[9]

In 1909, a Defence Act brought in compulsory military training,

For King and country. Victor (seated in front) with his three brothers before the war, left to right, Herbert, Julian and Reginald.

Christophers family archive

Anzac troops ashore at Gallipoli on 25 April 1915. Vic and the Otago machine gunners would follow the main force two weeks later.

Australian National War Memorial Library

providing for a Territorial Force (TF) of 30,000 men. The dominion's armed forces were reorganised and by 1914 the country had a field army of two infantry divisions (one in each island) and two mounted rifles brigades, supported by artillery batteries, reserves and coastal defence units. Among the array of new units was the Otago Mounted Rifles Regiment, in which Vic Christophers was soon to enlist.

By now, the four Christophers boys were at work and the threat of a major European war was steadily growing. On 28 June 1914, the fuse was lit when Archduke Franz Ferdinand, heir to the throne of Austria-Hungary, was assassinated by Serbian nationalists in the city of Sarajevo. Backed by Germany, the Austro-Hungarians declared war against Serbia, ostensibly in retaliation for the murder of the Austrian archduke.

Russia then mobilised in support of its fellow Slavs, the Serbs. Germany saw this as a hostile act against its ally, Austria-Hungary, and immediately declared war on Russia. At the same time the Germans invaded neutral Belgium and northern France in an attempt to defeat the French before turning their armies against the Russians in the east. Britain was drawn into the conflict by its role as guarantor of the neutrality of Belgium and fears for its security should the European continent fall under German control.

The underlying causes of the Great War were complex, involving the conflicting ambitions and rivalries of two opposing alliances—the Triple Entente of Russia, France and Britain, and the Central Powers, Germany, Austria-Hungary and Turkey. Germany wanted an empire that would match its growing military and industrial power, and had embarked upon a massive naval shipbuilding programme. The British saw this as a threat to their supremacy at sea, and responded with a naval build-up of their own.

The French nursed grievances against Germany as a result of their defeat in the Franco-Prussian war of 1870–71 and the subsequent loss of the coal and iron-rich region of Alsace-Lorraine. The Russians had ambitions of their own in the Balkans as champion of the Slav races then under the control of the Austro-Hungarian Empire. Added to this was Germany's fear of encirclement by the three entente powers, and Britain's fear that German domination of the continent would threaten its security. By 1905, Germany had replaced France and Russia as the British Empire's most likely future enemy.

The New Zealand Government's response to the declaration of war on 4 August, 1914 was swift. Immediately, it cabled London with the offer of an expeditionary force of one infantry brigade, a mounted rifles brigade, an artillery brigade and support units—the first such pledge from all of Britain's dominions. The offer was accepted on 12 August, and immediately the call went out for volunteers.

Men from all trades and professions rushed to join up, 14,000 in the first week alone. Training camps were set up in Auckland, Palmerston North, Wellington, Christchurch and Dunedin, and cargo and passenger ships requisitioned for conversion into troopships. "Men of peace clamoured in their thousands to enroll," wrote a local historian in the fevered prose of the time. "Never did fiery cross on highland hill stir the fighting blood of the clansmen as did the call for men stir the soul of young New Zealand."[10] "War!" thundered a New Zealand Herald editorial. "There is no conception more inspiring, no condition nobler, no call that rings more grandly in the ears."

They joined up for a mix of motives—the serious-minded for King and country, others to test their courage in battle, or as an outlet for natural aggressions. Most, however, enlisted for travel and adventure, and the chance to escape the constrictions of life in post-Victorian New Zealand. At work were years of indoctrination in the values of patriotism and loyalty to the British Empire through Boy Scouts, school cadets, and the Volunteer Force; "imperialist" politicians, the Church and the Press.

At work also was a "martial mythology" that by 1914 had given the soldier an iconic status in the public imagination. In Britain and in New Zealand also a culture dominated by "utilitarianism, industrialism, materialism, and urban squalor" was giving way to romantic visions of "clean, heroic and virtuous individualism." Exemplifying these virtues was the soldier—"a modern knight who embodied noble ideals, would fight for justice, display martial valour and, if necessary, sacrifice to fulfil his duty."[11]

The men who joined up in 1914, however, understood little of the wider causes of the conflict, and because there had been no major European war since 1815 they had inherited an essentially romantic view of warfare. War was about glory and sacrifice, the ultimate test of manliness, they had been told by their teachers and church leaders. Their duty was to defend Britain and the empire against its enemies, against whom they were expected to prevail in a short and victorious war.

As a result, their generation was profoundly ignorant of what war between modern industrial states would entail. Military technology had improved dramatically in the 50 years since the end of the American Civil

War. Machine guns and quick-firing artillery would command the battlefield causing massive casualties, and tanks, aircraft, and submarines would make their first appearance in combat. Nearly 10 million men of all nations would die in the four years of fighting that followed or as a direct result of it. Over six million more would be seriously wounded.

In 1886, the year Vic was born, none of this could have been predicted. Vic grew from infancy into a black-haired, dark-complexioned youth, reflecting perhaps his mixed English and Portuguese ancestry. Like his brothers, Herbert ("Herb or Bertie"), Julian and Reginald ("Reg or Reggie"), he attended Southland Boys' High School, and like them excelled in almost all sports. Vic played for the school's First XV rugby and First XI cricket teams and was its athletics champion in 1902. Interestingly, for all these years he suffered from a bad stammer.

Academically, Vic was a high achiever, passing the Matriculation (later University Entrance) examination in senior school. A young man of well-developed literary tastes, he read the plays of George Bernard Shaw and the novels of H.G. Wells, Charles Dickens, Robert Louis Stevenson, Victor Hugo, Emile Zola, Thomas Hardy, George Eliot, and John Galsworthy. Among the poets he enjoyed were Robert Browning, Milton (Paradise Lost) and Matthew Arnold. There was evidence also of a developing interest in religious, scientific and philosophical subjects.

Thirty years later a university education might have been an option, followed by a career in the professions, but on leaving school Vic went to work for stock and station firm Wright Stephenson as a clerk. His employers described him as thoroughly competent, honest, sober and obliging, and in every way trustworthy. His decision to volunteer for overseas service, they observed, had occurred "just as his training and natural ability were beginning to be of value to us."

Having worked on up-country sheep and cattle stations during his vacations, Vic was an experienced horseman and so it was logical that his unit of choice should be the Otago Mounted Rifles Regiment (OMR). But entry into OMR or any unit of the New Zealand armed forces in 1914 was by no means guaranteed. Preference was given to single men and age limits were set between 20 and 34. No man under 5 feet 4 ins (1.62 metres) was accepted, and all had to undergo a standard medical examination.

Sight, hearing, heart and lungs, teeth and joints, were checked, the subject confirmed free of hernias, haemorrhoids, varicose veins and skin diseases, and confirmed as generally being of "good bodily and mental health." As a natural athlete, Vic had no trouble being passed fit for service, but some 40 per cent of the New Zealand-born volunteers who rushed the recruitment centres around the country in August 1914 would fail the test.

Nationwide, the mounted riflemen came from a mix of backgrounds, among them lawyers, teachers, students, bank workers, accountants, and clerical workers like Vic. Most, however, were from the country districts—shepherds, farmers and farm workers—men used to hard physical labour and working with horses.

As a trooper in the Otago Mounted Rifles, Vic was a member of a distinctive corps, starting with the uniform. The riflemen wore a slouch hat with a wide brim and a khaki tunic crossed by a leather ammunition bandolier and belt. Each man was equipped with a Lee Enfield rifle, bayonet, water bottle and haversack, iron rations, blankets, a day's grain ration for the horse, and other essential items of equipment. Including the rider, a troop horse might carry up to 130kg of weight on training exercises or into battle. In combat, the troopers fought in four-man sections. One man in each section held the horses while the other three fought on foot. The four men lived, worked, fought and sometimes died together, and they usually became close friends. So it was to be for trooper Vic Christophers.

Training for overseas deployment began almost immediately at Invercargill's Tahuna Park under the eye of Regimental Sergeant Major Sydney Wood, a former member of the British Dragoon Guards and a man of "ferocious mien and savage bark." The training at this stage, however, was basic—drill, physical exercises, fieldcraft and rifle shooting. Training to operational standard was to be provided once the New Zealand Expeditionary Force (NZEF) had disembarked in England and been integrated into British or Australian formations. "Discipline in all units was strict, but there was little offending," wrote mounted rifles brigade historian Terry Kinloch. "The risk of being left behind was sufficient to deter all but the most hardened criminal."[12]

After a hectic month of training, inspections, farewell parades, speeches and civic receptions, the Otago and Southland men sailed from Port Chalmers for Wellington. Here they would rendezvous with the New Zealand convoy that was bound for Western Australia, and ultimately—so it was thought—to England for further training and then service in France on the Western Front.

It was not to be, at least not yet. On arrival in Wellington, the entire force was ordered ashore because of fears by the Massey Government that the troopships might be intercepted in the Tasman by a powerful German naval squadron under Vice-Admiral von Spee. The expeditionary force would now await the arrival of a strong naval escort of British and Japanese warships. Animals, artillery and stores were unloaded and hasty camps set up around Wellington. Training continued ashore while the city took on the look of a garrison town as soldiers thronged the streets, refreshment rooms, and hotels.

By 14 October the naval escorts had arrived and the horses, troops, their guns and equipment were re-embarked. On the morning of the 16th, 8454 men and 3818 horses of the NZEF, under the command of Major General Alexander Godley, sailed slowly through Wellington Harbour heads and out into the Tasman. A crowd of up to 50,000 had greeted the troops as they marched from their Karori camp to the ships. Out on the harbour, bands played while 1000 or more gathered at the Wellington heads to see the men on their way.

Ironically, the delay changed the course of the war for the entire NZEF, and for Vic himself. Had the force sailed as intended at the end of August or early September it would probably have reached England before Turkey entered the war in early November. Instead of fighting at Gallipoli for most of 1915, the New Zealanders would most likely have been deployed, after further training in England, to face the Germans on the Western Front.

Getting to their destination involved a seven-week voyage, first to Hobart in Tasmania then on to King George Sound in Western Australia to link up with the troopships carrying the 20,000 troops of the Australian Infantry Force (AIF). Aboard ship, the troopers exercised and groomed their horses, cleaned out their stalls, and with their animals endured the miseries of seasickness as the convoy headed west for its rendezvous with the Australians.

While the troops were still at sea, Turkey entered the war on the side of the Central Powers. Now allied with Germany, the Turks were seen to pose a threat to British control of the Suez Canal, and so the convoy was diverted to Egypt. There, it was planned, they would train together before going on to the Western Front in the spring of 1915.

On 3 December, after narrowly avoiding the German raider *Emden*, the New Zealand troops came safely ashore at Alexandria and entrained for Zeitoun, a desert camp north-west of Cairo. In future years, the survivors would recall with mixed feelings the seven-week voyage from home—the exotic sights of Ceylon's capital Colombo, the filth and squalor of Alexandria, the long train trip through the fertile Nile Delta to their camp at Zeitoun. Now they would have their first encounter with the land of the Old Testament with its minarets, great pyramids, heat, dust and everlasting sand.

Training began almost immediately as Godley wanted his New Zealanders ready for active service by February. For the mounted men there was trench digging, practice in musketry, dismounting at the gallop and advancing on foot under cover of machine gun and artillery fire. Their commander, Brigadier General Andrew Russell, a Hawke's Bay farmer, taught his men to swim their horses safely across the Nile.

On 18 December, Egypt was declared a British protectorate. Five days later, a force of Anzac and British troops, including the Otago Mounted Rifles, rode through the streets of Cairo to mark the event and to deter any nationalist elements in the population that might be tempted to challenge British authority.

Then at last the promise of action. A mixed Turkish and Arab force was reported to be advancing into Egypt to threaten British control of the Suez Canal. In the ensuing action, the 25,000-strong enemy force was heavily repulsed while attempting to cross the canal. Men of the New Zealand Infantry Brigade took part in the battle but the mounteds were not required. Vic, as keen as any of his comrades for action, was yet to have his first taste of battle.

After four months of hard desert training, Godley was now satisfied that the New Zealand and Australian contingents had been transformed from an army of raw citizen-soldiers into a force of well-trained and disciplined fighting men. He wrote to Minister of Defence James Allen: "You have here a force of 11,000 well-trained men of splendid physique, nearly all fit, beautifully mounted, thoroughly well-equipped, and ready, and only too willing, to go and fight for the Empire."[13]

Meanwhile, the War Office in London was devising a campaign to break the military stalemate on the Western Front by opening a second front against Germany's ally Turkey in the east. Under this plan a combined British and French naval force would break through the Dardanelles Straits into the Sea of Marmara to threaten the Turkish capital Constantinople (Istanbul). This, it was hoped, would force the Turkish Government to sue for peace and withdraw from its alliance with Germany and Austria-Hungary.

The capitulation of Turkey would open a supply route through the Black Sea, allowing military supplies to reach the Russian armies fighting the Germans and Austrians in the east. Greece, Bulgaria and Romania would be encouraged to join the Allied Triple Entente, and Russia, by a secret agreement with the British Government, would take control of Armenia and the Turkish capital Constantinople.

The War Office plan envisaged that 16 British and French battleships, supported by cruisers and destroyers, would steam up the Dardanelles Straits, bombarding and destroying the Turkish gun emplacements onshore while a flotilla of minesweepers cleared the water ahead of them. Once the fleet was through the Narrows, it would work its way through the Sea of Marmara and on to Constantinople.

It was a disaster. On March 18, Turkish mines and shore gunfire put a third of the fleet out of action, sinking four of the battleships and drowning hundreds of British and French sailors. The navy had failed; the job would now have to be finished by the soldiers in a shore landing against now much-strengthened Turkish defences.

The first dominion troops sailed from Egypt for the Dardanelles on 10 April as the newly-formed Australian and New Zealand Army Corps (Anzac). Temporarily left behind were the mounted regiments whose horses could not operate in Gallipoli's rugged terrain. The mounteds cheered the infantry as they entrained for Alexandria and the ships that would take them to the Dardanelles, but most were desperate not to miss the fight. Some even talked of deserting their units and joining their mates, among them machine-gunner Vic Christophers.

Their time, however, was soon to come. In early May, the Gallipoli force commander, Lieutenant General Sir William Birdwood, called for reinforcements to build up Anzac infantry battalions that had suffered heavy casualties in the initial landings on 25 April. The New Zealand Mounted Rifles Brigade, plus a brigade of Australian Light Horse, was ordered to Gallipoli. With them would go Vic and the Otago machine gunners, commanded by Lieutenant Allan Finlayson.

On 12 May, 3000 men of the 1st Australian Light Horse brigade, under Colonel Harry Chauvel, and the New Zealand Mounted Rifles, under Brigadier General Andrew Russell, arrived safely off Anzac Cove. The troopers crowded the rails trying to identify signs of battle ashore and the positions of the Anzac battalions that had landed on 25 April. As darkness fell, destroyers and torpedo boats came alongside and transferred the men to the barges that would be towed by small boats into shore. Every man was well loaded—rifle and bayonet, 200 rounds of ammunition; water bottle and rations; blankets, waterproof sheet, overcoat, spare clothes and toilet kit.

By now, the Gallipoli campaign was into its third week. The Anzacs had landed at a point called Ari Burnu after an error by the Royal Navy had put them ashore one-and-a-half kilometres too far to the north. Instead of facing what they believed would be lightly-defended Turkish positions in relatively open country, 16,000 Australian and New Zealand troops were pinned down on two narrow ridges above the beachhead, fighting off fierce Turkish counter-attacks.

Mixed groups of Australians and New Zealanders had pushed inland, only to be cut off and killed. Under murderous shrapnel and sniper fire, others had retreated to the beach or found shelter in steep gullies. The attacking battalions were steadily forced back to a line of outposts that would form their front line for the next eight months—Courtney's Post, Quinn's Post, Steele's Post, Pope's Hill and Walker's Top. From Cape Helles to Ari Burnu, the Allied advance had been held; the assault of 25 April had become a siege. Total Anzac casualties were now 8500, of whom some 2300 had been killed.

Meanwhile, the two mounted brigades were confronted with the realities of the Gallipoli campaign—men, animals and supplies crowded into a narrow beachhead, machine gun and rifle bullets whining overhead, freshly dug graves in a makeshift cemetery nearby. After an uncomfortable night, they climbed up to Walker's Top where they took over a section of the front line from men of the Royal Naval Division. Walker's Top was exposed on all sides to the higher Turkish trenches and every loophole had been targeted by snipers. Out in No Man's Land lay the unburied bodies of Turks and Anzacs, casualties of the previous two-and-a-half weeks of fighting.

Russell put his 1500 mounted riflemen quickly to work. The track bringing guns and supplies up to their position was widened and two 18-pounder guns dragged up onto Walker's Top. Saps were driven out into No Man's Land to give the troops a clear field of fire, and shelters cut into the trench walls where the men could rest and sleep in safety. Rolls of barbed wire were put in place to protect their positions against frontal attack and wire netting to shield them against Turkish bombs and grenades. Sandbag barricades were built to conceal tracks from Turkish snipers and countermining under Turkish trenches was begun.

From the start, the Turkish snipers hunted the Anzac machine gunners relentlessly, and the Otago men were quick to suffer. Two of Vic's mates were shot through the head while sitting at their guns. Then on the night of 18–19 May, 42,000 Turks charged the entire front line, howling "Allah! Allah!" as they came. In their trenches and saps, the Anzacs poured a devastating fire into the advancing waves, and after repeated attacks over 10,000 Turks lay dead or wounded between the lines. Some 630 Anzacs were also killed, among them 60 of Russell's mounted men.

Vic Christophers and the Otago machine gunners at No. 2 Outpost were unscathed that night as most of the fighting took place on Russell's Top and further south. Small enemy parties bore down on the outposts at the beginning and end of the main attack but were driven off. On 23 May, Vic wrote home, the tone of his letter upbeat and reassuring. Significantly, it made no mention of the slaughter just a few nights before.

"My dear Mother, Father–

I am writing this during a halt on the way to a new position. It is a lovely summer morning 8.30am. I would still be in bed if I were at home. We were up at 4.30 this morning. We are just beside the sea and are camped in a picturesque spot, reminding me of Stewart Island. I cannot sleep comparing the beauty of our surroundings, the lovely sunsets, the calmness of the sea with the death struggle we are engaged in. If Mother were here she might say with a good deal of satisfaction: 'Where every prospect pleases and only man is vile.'

"The life is sometimes strenuous, you get tired with continual work and lack of sleep, but when we get a spell life is very pleasant. It is just like a picnic. We get a swim in the sea nearly every day. You soon get used to the shells… You learn to know when they are coming your way by the singing sound you hear. When they sound close you dive for the nearest cover. You do not feel half as nervous as you would suspect when going under fire for the first time.

"The Turks were dropping a few odd sheets of shrapnel when we were landing. I had the same sort of feeling I often have had when going to the dentist. You get used to it and learn not to cry out before you are hurt. But we are having a rosy time compared with those who landed first, they had a very hard time of it. The account I wrote while at Alexandria of the landing of the colonials is fairly correct. I am forbidden to say any more about it now. You will understand I cannot write anything with regard to our operations. I have seen the place our fellows stormed, mostly all landslips, and the taking of that is equal to any feat I have ever read of British warfare.

"I met George Tothill last night, he was wounded in the leg, he's quite well again now. It is remarkable how few wounds are serious. You need not worry if I am ever posted as wounded, very few die from wounds. I have just heard that I am supposed to have been shot. Some of our fellows arrived a few days ago and I met some of them this morning. Eric Davidson from the Bluff has been congratulating me on being alive. Of course it is just another rumour. We are always hearing of the death of someone (and) meeting them a few days after. None of our section have been hurt yet.

"We are camped in a very healthy spot, there is very little sickness. This is much healthier than Cairo… We are very well fed here, better than we were since leaving NZ. We get supplied with tobacco and matches and get rum served out twice a week. We don't think much of the prohibitionists who want to stop our rum and beer. It is the one luxury we have. I have never met a prohibitionist in the Army."

The reality of the Gallipoli campaign was much different. Turkish snipers, shellfire and machine gun fire were a daily experience for Vic and his mates, along with the constant fear that the Turks would break the Anzac line and drive them into the sea. Thirst, poor food, lice infestations and disease made life a further test of endurance. As infantryman Leonard Thompson put it: "We were all lousy and we couldn't stop shitting because we had caught dysentery. We wept, not because we were frightened, but because we were so dirty."[14]

Four days after the Turkish attack, the two sides agreed to an armistice to bury the dead—Turks, Australians and New Zealanders. The corpses lay so thick in the scrub in front of the Anzac trenches that it was almost impossible to pass without treading on hideously swollen bodies, or avoid the stench that made men want to vomit.

Three days later, Vic and his fellow Anzacs watched in shock as a German submarine sank the battleship *Triumph* in full view of both armies. Two days later the same submarine repeated the feat, sinking the old battleship *Majestic* off Cape Helles. British Rear-Admiral Sir John de Robeck, commander of the naval force in the Dardanelles, withdrew all his larger ships to the island of Imbros, leaving the Anzac forces with only the minimum of naval support.

The Otago men were to be active again in the rescue of Canterbury and Wellington troopers from an ill-conceived attack on Turkish trenches

Show of force. The NZ Mounted Brigade rides through Cairo after landing in Egypt in December 1914.

Australian National War Memorial Library

in front of No. 2 Outpost. Under a hail of Turkish shrapnel, Vic and the other machine gunners covered the withdrawal of the survivors and fought off the Turkish counter-attack that followed close behind.

At 1.30am on 30 June, the Turks made a last attack on the Anzac line, but were again repulsed with heavy losses. "In the moonlight, the Turk, calling on his God, surged forward to the attack on No.4 section," wrote campaign historian Major Fred Waite. "In the half light the machine gunners found the range and mercilessly cut up the attacking waves. But they were not to be denied. On and on they pressed, right up to the parapets."[15]

Among the mounted brigade's few casualties was trooper Vic Christophers, shot dead by a Turkish sniper as he stood to his gun. Vic's mates took it hard, among them trooper Rupert Pyle who told his family how it happened. "Turkish snipers were plugging at our chaps all day. A head a bit too high meant, as a rule, sudden death! An early and much lamented victim of enemy marksmen was poor old Vic Christophers who was shot dead up in the trenches we were in last night. I was talking to him just before I left. They got him this morning. Vic's death is hard on anyone who knew him. He was one of the best chaps I ever knew and us fellows who were pals of his are very cut up. There are so many good fellows gone though."[16]

Trooper Ernie Royd wrote to his mother: "Poor dear old Vic, how we all miss him; I can't say what a loss he is to me, he was the only fellow in the section I could speak to freely. Now his body lies at the foot of our little hill, with another of our small gun team beside him. Vic and I never did agree upon souls, but if there is a place for them I guess he's near the top of the class with a place in the sun."[17]

The Gallipoli campaign effectively destroyed the Otago Mounted Rifles as a unit. By the time it ended with the evacuation of the Anzac force in mid-December, 130 troopers had been killed and nearly 270 wounded. Many others had suffered serious illness or were to be psychologically damaged for the rest of their lives. From these trials at least Vic Christophers would be spared.

Herbert Henry ("Herb") Christophers.

3

HERBERT HENRY ("HERB")

They told me Heraclitus,
They told me you were dead.
They brought me bitter news to hear
And bitter tears to shed.

— Callimachus on the death of his friend Heraclitus.
Translated from the Greek by William Johnson Cory

Herbert ("Herb") Christophers was born in Dunedin on 22 October, 1888. Like his older brother Victor, he had dark hair and an olive complexion and was of medium height. Like all of his brothers, Herb attended Southland Boys' High School, served in the school cadets, and was a prominent athlete, playing for both the Invercargill football and cricket clubs.

Herb began his working life as a draftsman in the railway engineers' office in the central North Island town of Ohakune. Like Victor, he enlisted immediately on the outbreak of war and in August 1914 sailed with the New Zealand expeditionary force that would seize German-occupied Samoa at the request of the British Government.

Commanded by Lieutenant Colonel Robert Logan, the 1360-strong occupation force included three companies of infantry, a battery of field artillery, railway engineers, and technicians from New Zealand Post and Telegraph. Because a German naval squadron was known to be operating somewhere in the Pacific, the two troopships were given a strong naval escort—five French and Australian light cruisers and the battlecruiser HMAS *Australia*.

The expeditionary force arrived off the capital, Apia, on 29 August, but the German authorities decided to offer no resistance. By early evening, the troops had been landed, stores unloaded and Government buildings,

Troops of the New Zealand expeditionary force sent to capture German Samoa in August 1914. Lieutenant Herb Christophers commanded the engineers detachment responsible for maintaining rail communications on the island.

Christophers family archive

The result of German bombardment—a ruined cathedral in the Belgian city of Ypres. The New Zealanders at Armentieres, where Herb first saw action, would suffer heavy casualties from enemy gunnery.

RSA Collection. Alexander Turnbull Library

A front-line trench in France about 1916. Herb Christophers and his fellow officers lived in dugouts carved out below the trench line. The troops slept in damp, rat-infested burrows cut into the trench walls.

RSA Collection. Alexander Turnbull Library.

including the post office telegraph exchange, seized. A party dispatched to capture the island's wireless station, however, arrived too late. The Germans had already sabotaged much of the station's equipment rendering it inoperative.

As force commander, Logan read the proclamation banning public meetings, ordering all firearms to be handed in, and introducing a rigid night-time curfew. German officials were sent to New Zealand to be imprisoned on Motuihe Island in Auckland's Hauraki Gulf or on Soames Island in Wellington Harbour.

As a lieutenant in command of the engineers, Herb Christophers was responsible for the railway that had been built by the Germans from Apia to the wireless station. His immediate task was to improve the existing line and lay extensions to the New Zealand camp on the island. As a first step, a small petrol locomotive, capable of hauling 10 tons of freight, was put back into operation after being disabled by the Germans.

The occupation could well have been short-lived. Von Spee's German naval squadron arrived off Apia on 14 September, just three days after the New Zealanders' naval escort had departed. The Germans, however, decided to take matters no further, apparently because they feared damage to German property on the island should their ships open fire. Instead, the vice-admiral turned his heavy cruisers towards the French possession of Tahiti, which he bombarded before heading for South America.

The expeditionary force was to remain on Samoa until relieved in April 1915, but some of its members were to win notoriety for their behaviour during the occupation. On Christmas Eve 1914, New Zealand soldiers broke out of camp and into three hotels in Apia. When the proprietor refused to sell them liquor, they grabbed bottles of drink and subsequently ransacked a warehouse of whiskey and brandy.

Predictably, the Press at home, operating under wartime censorship, made no mention of this episode. The Southland Boys' High School magazine reported only that prominent old boy Lieutenant H.H. Christophers had returned from Samoa "thin and bronzed" after contracting dengue fever and suffering "much debility and persistent pains." The magazine noted, however, that he had made a full recovery.

Herb now married Mamie Dodds, daughter of an orchardist from Paraparaumu just north of Wellington. There are no details of their courtship or of Mamie Dodds herself, but just months after the wedding ceremony Herb enlisted again for overseas service and was posted to 2 Battalion New Zealand Rifle Brigade for training. Herb was about to board his troopship in Wellington when his mother Juliet, who was there to see him off, received news of the death of his brother Vic at Gallipoli. It was just eight-and-a-half months since Vic had sailed with his mounted regiment for Egypt.

After training in Egypt, Herb sailed with the newly formed New Zealand Division for France with the rank of captain and under the command of Major General Sir Andrew Russell, now newly knighted and promoted. As enemy submarines were known to be active in the Mediterranean, the troops were ordered to wear lifebelts night and day as several ships had been torpedoed the day before the convoy sailed. The division, however, arrived at the port of Marseilles without incident and entrained for Armentières in northern France.

By the time the New Zealanders arrived in France the war was 20 months old. On 4 August 1914, German forces had crossed the border into Belgium and northern France with the aim of swiftly defeating the French before turning their full force against Russia in the east. The Germans, however, were held by the French at the Battle of the Marne and the two forces—Allied and German—were locked in a stalemate on what was now the Western Front. Both armies had built opposing systems of trenches that stretched some 730 kilometres from the North Sea to the Swiss Alps.

By the end of 1915, British attempts to break through German defences at Neuve Chapelle, Aubers Ridge, Festubert and Loos had cost their armies some 285,000 casualties. The British high command, however, had ambitious plans for 1916 in the form of a combined French and British offensive on the Somme in July. This, it was hoped, would break the stalemate on the Western Front and take the pressure off French forces at Verdun where a massive German offensive was attempting to draw in and ultimately destroy the French Army.

Meanwhile, the New Zealand Division was to relieve the British 17th Division on a six-kilometre section of the line in front of Armentières, a grim little manufacturing town on the Franco-Belgian border. The sector was a "quiet" one, which would give the New Zealanders time to become familiar with the terrain and conditions of northern France, and the tactics of their German enemy, before being committed to offensive operations. Most of all it would give the still raw troops time to improve the skills they needed to survive and fight effectively on the Western Front.

On 19 April, Herb wrote to his younger brother Quintin from a village just outside Armentières: "Well we landed quite safe (in Marseilles) after an uneventful voyage, saw no submarines but were visited three or four times by patrol boats and once by an Italian destroyer. Two of us are quartered in a most comfortable house with lovely soft beds, hardships of war missing!

"We see very little of the people of the house tho' and mess with several other officers about 5 minutes' walk away. I would rather have fed in the house as then we would have had a good opportunity to pick up some French. We heard guns the day we arrived but haven't heard them since… Otherwise we haven't seen or heard much of the war."

For the New Zealanders, many of whom were veterans of Gallipoli, the Western Front was strange and in other ways familiar. Gallipoli's trenches had been dug from dry soil. Here they had to be excavated from water-sodden flats and protected by breastworks built up above ground level and reinforced with sandbags, wooden stakes, and corrugated iron. For northern France was low-lying, the water table high, and heavy shellfire tended to turn it into a morass of mud.

The routine, however, was soon to become familiar—sentry duty at night, the stand-to at dawn, the sleeping in boots and clothes, the everlasting fight against lice and rats. There was the incessant work—mostly under cover of night—bringing up food and ammunition; digging or improving trenches, dugouts and gun emplacements; building parapets and listening posts, and erecting and repairing wire entanglements. At night, small patrols crept out into No Man's Land to cover the wiring parties and check the position of the enemy trenches, and in these, Herb Christophers would have taken an active part. The best of the junior officers led by example and too often they paid for it with their lives or, if they survived, by being quickly burnt out.

When in the front line, Herb and his fellow officers slept in sparsely appointed dugouts, the troops in "damp, lousy, rat-infested" burrows excavated from the trench walls. Their German enemy was seldom sighted—a grey shadow seen above a trench for a few seconds in daylight, a head and shoulders seen through a sniper's loophole, "wraiths in spiked helmets" scuttling for cover during a night raid, the blue smoke of their breakfast fires in the morning.[18]

Day and night the division's artillery pounded enemy ammunition dumps, billets, and parapets as part of a broader strategy to stop the Germans shifting troops south to the Somme where a new offensive was soon to begin. Raids were mounted on their trenches to capture prisoners and identify German units, and to maintain the aggressive spirit of troops fighting a largely static war.

Captain Wilkes, one of Herb's fellow officers, wrote home: "During the time we have been in the trenches we have ruffled old Fritz properly, and he has found out that the Anzacs are not prepared to sit still. In short, we have given him 'What ho', and, of course, getting some change back ourselves. We have had all sorts of experiences crowded into the few weeks we have been here, but of course, the grand one is yet to come, when we go forward with the bayonet."

Lieutenant Colonel "Curly" Blyth, then a private in Herb's brigade, put it more bluntly: "The Huns and the British forces had sort of come to an arrangement not to hurt one another… But we hadn't travelled 12,000 miles to sit on our backsides and wait for the Germans. So it wasn't long before the Rifle Brigade started to raid the German trenches. The Germans retaliated and it deteriorated into just another part of the line, with the result that when we left to go to the Somme in '16, the French said that they would sooner have the Huns than those black-button bastards from New Zealand."[19]

The Armentières period was a costly one for the New Zealand Division as raids and night patrols, snipers, machine guns and shellfire took a steady toll of men's lives. In its three months manning a so-called "quiet" sector of the line, the division suffered 2500 casualties and left some 600 dead behind in the cemeteries of that shattered town. Among them was Herb Christophers, killed in his trench by an exploding bomb on 2 June.

Writing home, Captain Wilkes told his family how it happened: "Captain Christophers had charge of several fatigues (working parties), which were carrying on in our front line. Fritz sent over a number of shells, bombs etc. in retaliation for a big strafing we had given him all day. 'Chris' walked along the trench yarning to the men and refused to take cover. He would have been safe had he stayed in the bays, but he went along a travel trench, and then a cluster of bombs came over into the trenches just ahead of him. He knelt down and took cover, but one landed just in front of him and the blow-back killed him instantaneously.

"It was not noticed at first that he had been killed, as he never altered the kneeling position he had taken up. Young Hare, who used to be in the Railway Department at Riverton, was alongside of him when it happened, and was wounded in the eye by the same bomb. Peter Scully got a slight shell wound in the forehead. According to 'young Hare', Herb's last words were, 'Get nearer to me or you will get hit.'"

Herb was buried in Cite Bon Jean Military Cemetery outside Armentières on 3 June. On 14 August, Russell handed over his sector to the 51st Highland Division and entrained his division for the Somme. In the three weeks of bloody fighting that followed the New Zealand Division would lay the foundations of its reputation as one of the finest in the British Army. The cost would be nearly 8000 officers and men killed and wounded, equivalent to eight of its 12 battalions. Herb Christophers would now be just one among many.

Julian Anthony Christophers.

4

JULIAN ANTHONY

What passing-bells for these who die as cattle?
Only the monstrous anger of the guns.

– World War I soldier-poet Wilfred Owen

Julian Christophers was born in Dunedin on 28 May 1884, the second of Anthony and Juliet's five sons. He was short—just over 5 feet tall (1.52 metres)—strongly built, with dark-brown hair and an olive complexion. Like his brothers, he was educated at Southland Boys' High School where he excelled in rugby, cricket and rowing. He captained the school's First XI cricket team for two years and played on the wing for its First XV. As the Southland Times put it: "Private Christophers developed early into a particularly fine specimen of vigorous manhood, keenly devoted to rowing and football in which his powerful physique stood him in good stead."

On leaving school, Julian joined the Invercargill Rowing Club, enjoying "almost unbroken success" as a member of its maiden, junior and senior crews. In rugby, he excelled again, captaining the Invercargill Football Club's senior team and representing Southland Province for two seasons as an outstanding rugby three-quarter. A serious knee injury during a major game put a premature end to his football career; it should have ruled him out of active military service altogether.

Like his brother Victor, Julian's first job on leaving school was with stock and station firm Wright Stephenson. At the time he was also serving in the Volunteer Force with the rank of sergeant. In April 1908 he married Earle Bremner and they had one child, Juliet, born in 1909. There is no record of their time together, or about Earle herself, but by 1916 they were living

F. Miller (Cox.)   R. G. Christophers (2.)   J. A. Christophers (Stroke.)
T. Brown (3.)   A. Arthur (Bow.)

WINNERS YOUTHS FOURS, INVERCARGILL REGATTA, 1903.

Invercargill Rowing Club.

Julian (right standing) and his brother Reg (left standing). Julian excelled in all sports, and particularly in rowing and senior rugby. A serious knee injury put an end to his rugby playing career, but should have ruled him out of military service altogether.

Christophers family archive

A German pillbox captured by the New Zealanders. Strong points like these inflicted heavy casualties on troops of the Canterbury Battalion at Polderhoek Chateau where Julian was fatally wounded.

RSA Collection. Alexander Turnbull Library

at Wairoa in northern Hawke's Bay, where Julian managed a branch of the stock and station firm Dalgety and Co.

Three months after the bloodbath on the Somme, Julian volunteered for military service and was passed physically fit despite the knee injury that had put an end to his rugby-playing days. An undated note on his personnel record reads: "This soldier is certified M/U (militarily unfit) for service in and beyond New Zealand, but it is evident a mistake was made by the medical officer. No further action is necessary meanwhile."

Julian's letters to his younger brother Quintin that year make it clear that he was determined to serve, despite his knee injury, the deaths of his two brothers in action, and the fact that his wife and child would be left alone for a year or more, perhaps forever. On 12 June, he wrote: "Sad news about Bertie (Herb). Do write and tell me how mother and father are. Poor little Mamie will be very sad too… Let me know at once if you have enlisted yet, because now you must stay at home, at present anyhow. My knee seems better, and if strong enough, it is my turn to go next, and I intend to go. Do not say anything (yet) to mother and father."

On 18 December, just days after he had volunteered for overseas service, Julian told Quintin: "I do not like breaking up my happy home, but every sacrifice has to be made these days… Perhaps my leg will not stand active service, and I am half afraid I will be chucked out in camp."

Meanwhile, the War Council in London was planning another major offensive in France and asked the New Zealand Government to send an extra division of troops (10–12,000 men) or at least a brigade. Massey reluctantly agreed to another brigade but only if it was composed of existing reinforcements in England. Massey made it clear that New Zealand would send no more than 100,000 men to the front. "There is a growing feeling in NZ," Minister of Defence James Allen wrote in October 1917, "that the willing horse is being bled to death."[20]

Supporting the New Zealand Government's case was the fact that the country was already reinforcing at a proportionately higher rate than the other British dominions—2200 a month for its single division compared, for example, to Australia's 1400 per month for each of its five divisions. The entry of the United States into the war in April, it was argued, made it unnecessary for New Zealand to go on stretching itself to the limit. By 1918, the final year of the war, the reinforcement rate would drop from 27,650 in 1917 to just 9650. Among the men accepted for service in these last two years would be brothers Julian and Reg Christophers.

Julian joined 1 Battalion Canterbury Infantry Regiment as a private. Given his obvious leadership abilities, including the captaincy of Southland Boys' High School's First XI and the Invercargill Football Club's senior team, he should logically have been selected for officer training. In the event, he joined the regiment in the ranks and, perhaps by choice, would remain there.

Julian left New Zealand with the 25th Reinforcements and went into training first at Sling Camp in Wiltshire—the largest of the camps for New Zealand troops in England—and then in the so-called Bull Ring at Etaples in France. On 26 July, he wrote to his brother Quintin: "The Canterbury Battalion has been kept in the Bull Ring ever since it arrived. Here we learn bayonet fighting, gassing, bomb throwing, wiring and the Lewis Gun. We start at 8am and finish at 5pm, march to and from the Bull Ring with field packs up, and march past the Camp Commandant every day… Everything in the Bull Ring is done at the double, so we are pretty tired in the evening. The Camp and everything in it is splendid," Julian assured his brother. "The food is very good and beautifully cooked."

The tone of the letter, however, reflected the confusion of that dark year when Allied morale was at its lowest: "People here are sanguine that the war will end soon. Now that America is in Germany will feel the economic pain. Returned men think it is almost impossible to break through in the West. Russia is upsetting things very much."

The Canterbury Regiment had been badly mauled the year before during the Third Battle of the Somme, its two battalions suffering over 1100 casualties in three weeks of fighting, and at Messines nine months later they had also lost heavily. Julian's introduction to service on the Western Front would come during the Third Battle of Ypres. The New Zealand Division's attack at Passchendaele on 12 October, in which his Canterbury Regiment was to play a key role, would be remembered as the bloodiest single day in New Zealand's military history.

On 22 July, the Third Battle of Ypres opened with the greatest artillery bombardment in the history of land warfare to date. On 31 July, the British and French forces attacked on a 25-kilometre front. By the end of the first day of the offensive the British 5th Army alone had lost more than a third of its strength in killed, wounded and missing. By the first week of October, Allied casualties had reached nearly 163,000.

Alarmed at the high cost for so little gain, Haig's two senior generals, Gough and Plumer, urged him to halt the offensive. Haig would not be moved. There were solid reasons still for carrying on, he argued—securing the positions already won, robbing the enemy of observation over the British line, and assisting the forthcoming French offensive on the Aisne. Enemy losses so far had also been severe and his morale was assumed to be low.

At this point Russell's New Zealand Division, including private Julian Christophers, joined the battle. At the Battle of Broodseinde on 4 October the New Zealanders gained all their objectives and took over 1100 prisoners, 60 machine guns and a large quantity of war material. If victory this time was relatively easy, it was again costly—over 1650 killed and wounded, many of them from the Canterbury Regiment.

On 5 October, the rain set in, turning the cratered battlefield into a lake and preventing artillery and essential supplies, including ammunition, from getting forward. Anxious to exploit the successes of 4 October, Haig instructed his commanders to continue with the offensive, at least until the Passchendaele ridge was secured.

For the attack on 12 October the 3rd Australian and the NZ Division would be used in tandem, supported by the British 9th Division. The aim was to strengthen the British hold on the ridge by capturing the village of Passchendaele and the Bellevue Spur to the north. The New Zealanders would take the spur; the Australians the village of Passchendaele itself.

On the morning of the 11th, Plumer was told that the formidable wire entanglements facing the New Zealand and Australian divisions could not be cut by shellfire in the 20 hours left before the attack. Something also had to be done about the hundreds of wounded men still stranded in the mud between the lines. Plumer was unmoved; the attack would go on.

For the New Zealand battalions the march up the night before in high winds and rain was a nightmare. Soaked and exhausted, Julian and his mates dug foxholes in the mud and waited in the dark for zero hour. Facing them on the high ground across No Man's Land was their objective, protected by dark rows of concrete bunkers, hidden machine-gun nests and thick belts of barbed wire.

At 5.30am, the artillery opened up but the creeping barrage was weak and patchy. With no stable platforms on which to rest, the guns tilted and sank into the mud and shells fell short, killing and wounding troops still in their assembly positions. Advancing to the attack, the Otago and Canterbury men were met with blasts of machine gun and artillery fire. Many were cut down almost as soon as they left their trenches; the rest came up against pillboxes protected by thick belts of uncut wire. Some reached the pillboxes only to be shot down before they could use their grenades.

Pinned down in front of the wire, the surviving troops were forced to go to ground. By now, over 840 men of the New Zealand Division were dead and some 2850 more were wounded or had been taken prisoner. For the Canterbury Regiment alone, the toll was 282 killed and 618 wounded. Not one of the division's objectives was taken.

Heavy rain and mud forced Haig to cancel the offensive the day after the failed Anzac assault, but the Canadian Corps was now ordered to finish the job. On 26 October, the remains of Passchendaele village finally fell to the Canadians at a cost of another 16,000 casualties.

For now, Julian Christophers had survived the holocaust unwounded, but two sets of brothers, the Stewarts and the Newloves, had not—all five killed in the attack of 12 October. For now, his shattered battalion would withdraw to positions in front of the ruined city of Ypres where the NZ Division would spend one of the harshest winters in the region on record.

By early December, Julian and his battalion would be in action again. Polderhoek Chateau, a kilometre from the Belgian village of Gheluvelt, was a heavily fortified German strongpoint flanked by lines of pillboxes. Four attacks by British units had so far failed to take the position and the Canterbury and Otago battalions were now ordered to take the ridge on which the ruins of the chateau stood.

From the start they would face an uphill struggle. The enemy's defences had been heavily bombarded in the week before the attack, but the main strongpoints had remained intact. The brigade commander then decided that the position would be taken by frontal assault rather than from the flank, which would expose his men to heavy machine-gun fire from the ridge. And while Julian was now a veteran of two major attacks, many of his comrades were untried reinforcements sent in to make up the losses suffered at Passchendaele. Both units were short of experienced officers and NCOs.

On 2 December, the Canterbury and Otago men formed up by the light of gun flashes for their four-hour march to the line. "On either side for miles the wreckage of a hundred fights still lies," wrote infantryman Norman Gray. "Dead horses, men, limbers, guns, tanks, all the impedimenta of an army embedded in a morass of mud, while through it all the narrow track still feeds the front with more men, more guns."[21]

The attack was a disaster from the beginning, a reprise of the assault at Passchendaele two months earlier. Shellfire from the supporting barrage fell amongst the first wave causing heavy casualties before it had properly begun. Shrapnel and high explosive from German artillery and intense machine-gun fire from the pillboxes on the ridge forced the rest to ground before they had advanced 200 metres. With both units now reduced to half strength, the brigade commander ordered his troops to dig in in front of the chateau.

On the night of 5 December, a British unit relieved the two New Zealand battalions, which pulled back to Howe Camp south-west of Ypres. The cost of the attack had been severe—100 killed and more than 300 wounded. Over 200 officers and men of 1 Canterbury Battalion alone were listed as killed, wounded or missing.

Among the dead was Private Julian Christophers. With shrapnel wounds in the stomach and both legs, he was taken to a casualty clearing station behind the line where he died without regaining consciousness. Within a week, the Germans retook the ground the New Zealanders had struggled at such high cost to capture. Polderhoek Chateau, wrote soldier-author John A. Lee who had witnessed the attack, was "the graveyard of men and hope."

In June 1931, Julian's widow Earle drove to Ypres to visit her husband's grave for the first time. In Lijssenthoek Military Cemetery—the last resting place of over 10,000 French, German, British and dominion soldiers—she laid a wreath of roses, peonies, and a red geranium. "It was so hard," she wrote home to his mother Juliet, "but I pulled my courage together and soon found my sweetheart's grave. It was strange, it didn't feel like Julian was there at all and he isn't I know, and that was a great big help and comfort. How wicked it all was, and seems to me so useless."

Reginald Gillon (Reg) Christophers.

5

REGINALD GILLON ("REG")

But I've a rendezvous with Death
At midnight in some flaming town,
When Spring trips north again this year,
And I to my pledged word am true,
I shall not fail that rendezvous.

— American soldier-poet Alan Seeger, killed on
the Western Front in 1916

Born in Dunedin on 8 August 1882, Reg was the oldest of the five sons of Anthony and Juliet Christophers. He began his schooling in Dunedin but finished it in Invercargill because his father Anthony was transferred to the Bank of New South Wales there when he was nine years old. Reg was the first of the five Christophers boys to attend Southland Boys' High School.

Described as "diligent and thorough in his duties," Reg, like all his brothers, was a prominent sportsman, playing for its First XI and captaining its First XV. He was active also in the school's cadet corps, and on leaving school joined the Volunteer Force where, like his brother Julian, he was promoted to the rank of sergeant at what was described as "an unusually early age."[22]

Reg opted for a career as a civil engineer and surveyor, serving first as a cadet in a firm of Invercargill civil engineers. He seemed destined to excel, topping the list for the country in the 1904 surveyor examinations and a year later was appointed an assistant surveyor with the New Zealand Government. In 1906, he emigrated to California where he worked for five years, helping to develop the State's expanding railway networks. Included was a two-month stint as a resident engineer for the construction of a section of the Western Pacific Railway, and surveying work for a large dam site being developed by the Sierra and San Francisco Power Company.

Reg in the uniform of the Volunteer Force before the war. "Diligent and thorough in his duties", Reg won promotion at an unusually early age.

Christophers family archive

Reg with sons Phillip and Cecil before sailing for England with the 34th Reinforcements in June 1918, the last year of the war.

Christophers family archive

Reg's wife Alice (centre), her two sons, and friends were on the wharf to farewell him as he boarded the troopship *Remuera*.

Christophers family archive

For King and country. The certificate of service that commemorated the sacrifice of 2nd Lieutenant Reginald Christophers in the Great War of 1914-1918. Issued by the Governor-General after the Armistice, it would have gone directly to his widow Alice as next of kin.

Christophers family archive.

Reg Christophers married Alice Mildred Vyner in Monterey, California, in August 1907, after she had sailed from New Zealand to join him. Again, little is known about Alice herself or about their courtship, but they were to have two children before the war, Phillip Anthony, born January 1909, and Cecil Gillon, born October 1913.

On his return to New Zealand in 1911, Reg went into private practice as a partner in the firm of Robinson and Christophers, consulting engineers to the Stratford Borough and other public organisations in the Taranaki province. In 1915, he was appointed engineer to the Dargaville-based Hobson County Council, based in the Far North town of Dargaville.

In June 1916 came the dreadful news that the second Christophers brother, Herb, had been killed in action on the Western Front. Reg wrote to an aunt: "It is very, very hard for poor mother and father. To see two sons, just in their young manhood, and who two years ago were following peaceful occupations, cut off, is a terrible trial for them. Theirs is the hardest part to play. For the boys themselves, they were good men, which is the only thing that really matters, and they died bravely fighting for a righteous cause."

As for himself, he told his aunt, he still aimed to enlist. "I have thought the matter over carefully; the side you mention is only one. On the other are the lives of my two brothers, and other dear friends who went expecting us to do our share after them. What an awful thing it would be for all the noble lives that have fallen that we, the living, did not see the thing through to the bitter end!"

Ironically, Reg Christophers volunteered for service overseas at a time when the supply of reinforcements for the New Zealand Division was about to be drastically scaled back. Behind this was the country's growing war weariness and a feeling within Massey's Government that New Zealand was paying too high a price in blood and money for its support of the British war effort. There were fears also that the dominion would run out of men before the end of the war if it continued to send reinforcements overseas at the current high rate.

Reg sailed for England with the 34th Reinforcements in June 1918, a voyage marked only by an encounter with a German submarine in the English Channel. From the troopship and from Sling Camp, he wrote affectionate letters to his son Cecil about tugs-of-war and playfights aboard ship; the squadrons of planes flying noisily over the camp and the anti-aircraft balloons tethered nearby; the porcupines, grey rabbits, doves and frogs he saw on walks in the countryside; about a little girl he had met called Margaret, who, like five-year-old Cecil, enjoyed being read to from *The Tales of Beatrix Potter*.

On 19 August, he wrote to older son Phillip from Sling Camp:

> My Dear Phillip
>
> I am now in a big camp in England and am learning a number of new things such as throwing bombs, erecting barbed wire entanglements and other things they use in real war. In fact there is (sic) a good many things just the same as real war. Yesterday we witnessed an attack made from the trenches just the same as the real one is, and a good deal of real ammunition was used. You might have liked to see the shells going off. We had to take care not to go too far up.
>
> There are many other camps around here with all kinds of soldiers in them. Last night I saw some artillery firing some star shells, which looked like pretty fireworks. There is also a hospital for wounded soldiers near here. We see some of them out for walks and really some do not look much older than you are.
>
> Perhaps you would have liked to see the fight our destroyers had with a real submarine the afternoon before we reached England. There were many real bombs fired, which made a great noise and shook our steamer. The destroyers rushed very fast through the water and homed very quickly…
>
> Thank you very much for your letters I received today and for the drawings of the badges, ships & warriors. I do not wear my badges at present at all but I hope to put up the machine gun badge again soon. Mother said you had been very kind to her getting morning tea for her on a Sunday.
>
> Good bye now old man.
>
> From Dad

After training at Sling and in the Bullring at Etaples, Reg joined 1 Battalion Otago Regiment as a second lieutenant in mid-September 1918. By now the New Zealand Division had been involved in several major actions critical to the Allied campaign on the Western Front. On 21 March, the "Kaiserschlact" offensive, a massive effort involving three German armies and 76 divisions, had begun in a last-ditch attempt to defeat the British and French before American troops arrived in strength on the Western Front. On 26 March, the New Zealanders had played a key role in plugging a six-kilometre gap in the British line through which German forces were moving to threaten a strategically vital railway junction at Amiens.

On 21 August, the New Zealand Division took its place in the front line of the "100 Days" advance by the Allied armies that would finally end the war on the Western Front. The division's opening assault on the village of Puisieux caught the German defenders by surprise, taking over 200 prisoners and 30 machine guns. It was the first of many such captures the division would make in the coming months.

On 24 August, the New Zealanders captured the villages of Grévillers and Biefvillers and swept the enemy from Loupart Wood. The next objective was the town of Bapaume, a struggle that would involve the division in one of the hardest-fought battles of its three years on the Western Front and one of its costliest. On 28 August, the Germans pulled out of Bapaume, harried by the New Zealanders who then forced them out of the villages of Bancourt and Fremicourt.

After the brutal trench fighting of the Somme, Messines and Passchen-daele, the division was now advancing across open country almost untouched by war—behind it a nightmare landscape of shell holes, barbed wire, wrecked villages and charred woods. Meanwhile, the enemy was making desperate efforts to delay the advancing Allied forces as it retreated across northern France and Belgium towards the German border. Villages, roads, railways and bridges were destroyed, key crossroads blown up and wells polluted, but the advance moved inexorably on.

By mid-September, the New Zealand Division had fought its way through Havrincourt Forest and Gouzeaucourt Wood towards the German Army's last line of defence, the "impregnable" Hindenburg Line. After a failed attempt to capture Trescault Ridge in two days of bloody fighting, the division went into reserve, emerging after a brief period of rest to join in the final phases of the advance.

On 1 October, the New Zealanders, now including Second Lieutenant Reg Christophers, forced a crossing of the St Quentin Canal to capture the village of Crévecoeur, holding it against heavy shelling and repeated coun-ter-attacks. On 8 October, the division was given a key role in the attack by the 3rd and 4th British armies on the heavily defended Masnieres-Beaurevoir Line. Supported by artillery barrages and large numbers of tanks, the New Zealanders attacked towards the village of Esnes at dawn. German artillery, machine guns and thick belts of wire held up the advance for a time but the enemy was eventually driven from his trenches and the village captured. Of the 1400 prisoners taken, 1 Otago Battalion took 100, a field gun and eight machine guns for the loss of 144 officers and men killed or wounded.

It was in this action that Reg Christophers' war came to an end. Brereton Williams, a fellow officer, wrote to his mother Juliet: "Reg got his wound like a hero leading his men through a gap in the wire on the Hindenburg Line. It was night-time and during the fight a Hun officer shot him in the neck." According to the doctor who attended him, Reg suffered very little pain, Brereton wrote. "His chief anxiety seemed to be what his dear mother might think, and he spoke frequently to the doctor of you." Reg died in a hospital behind the lines on 13 October. It was just four weeks after joining his regiment in the front line and a month before the Armistice that ended the war.

The news of the loss of a son, husband or other family member was usually delivered by boys on bicycles wearing Post Office uniforms. "Families feared the telegraph boy's bike—the riven household," wrote Ormond Burton, and again he had come. According to witnesses, Juliet rushed from her home at 12 Tweed St and collapsed in agony on the road outside. Neighbours who ran to help her found her holding up the telegram that told her that her oldest son, like the other three, had been killed in action.

Nearly 270,000 Allied soldiers would be killed or wounded in the "100 Days" offensive which ended the war on the Western Front. "The headstones in the comet's tail of cemeteries that trace the army's path from Santerre across to the Belgian border tell the story all too well," wrote war historian Richard Holmes.[23] Among them, in Beaulencourt British Cemetery, is that of Second Lieutenant Reginald Christophers, the last of four Invercargill brothers to die in World War I.

Of five brothers he was the single survivor. Quintin Gillon Christophers (seated centre) and his bride on their wedding day. At right are his now elderly parents Anthony and Juliet.

Christophers family archive

6

QUINTIN GILLON

God doth not need either man's work or his own gifts;
Who best bear his mild yoke, they serve him best.
His state is kingly. Thousands at his bidding speed
And post o'er land and ocean without rest:
They also serve who only stand and wait.

– English poet John Milton

Quintin, born in 1896, was the youngest of the five Christophers brothers and the only survivor of World War I. At school, he proved to be equally athletic as his brothers, playing for the senior rugby and cricket teams at Southland Boys' High School, and winning its singles tennis championship in 1912.

Family correspondence indicates that Quintin wanted to study for the priesthood in the Anglican Church after leaving school, but eventually followed his father into banking. As a long-term career it may not have been an easy fit. His daughter, Gwenda Birnie, recalled: "My father stammered for 40 years. The day he retired from the Hamilton branch of the Bank of New South Wales, he stopped stammering."

By September 1917, Quintin was serving in the Territorial Force and had finally been balloted for service overseas. He faced a difficult choice: obey the call-up without question or apply for an exemption. With his brothers serving overseas or living elsewhere in the country, he had a good reason for staying at home. He was—and had been for some time—sole carer for his two elderly parents.

On the death of Herb in June 1916, Reg had written to Quintin: "It must have been very hard for you to go home with the terrible news to the old people. The burden of looking after our parents has fallen mostly on your shoulders, and you have done much more than your share."

As for advice on what he should do about the call-up, Quintin's brothers seemed divided. Reg told him to listen to his conscience, not to the pro-enlistment messages in local newspapers or the opinions of the "man in the street." "Should you feel that your duty lies at home, I am quite sure that it is right and truly brave for you to stay. For myself, I feel that dear Bertie's death makes no difference. I shall go just as soon as I am accepted as an officer."

Julian wrote: "I am glad to hear that you are staying home in the meantime at least. If things get bad and men short, then I think you should go later on. It is very hard for old people, but still one's country should be considered first. Of course if Reg and I get away, then you must stay."

By February 1917 Julian was urging Quintin not to appeal if called up. Personally, he (Julian) would wait for the ballot and if called up would "just go." But if he and Reg were then in camp and it appeared that both of them would get away, he wrote, then it might be right for Quintin to appeal.

In November, the youngest of the Christophers brothers applied to the Military Appeal Board for an exemption and was eventually granted it. The grounds for his application are unknown, but are likely to have focused on his ongoing family responsibilities. Not yet could he claim to be the sole surviving son of a family in which at least one other son had been killed—the only other ground on which he would have been able to apply for an exemption from military service.

Of the board's decision, the *Southland Times* commented: "Of the four sons in the King's uniform, three have fallen in battle, a sacrifice which few families have been called on to make."

7

GROOMED FOR WAR

Then came the call to war. You knew he would want to go. The call of duty came to him, the call of his country, the call of com-radeship. Of course he must go… Was it not God's call to his soul? From that first opening of the eyes when he became a child up to the higher call to be a man and a patriot, and right on to the last call to lay down his life bravely, at its best?

– The *Church News* addresses parents of soldiers serving at Gallipoli in July 1915.

The Christophers were not the only Southland family to be shattered by the war. Equally hard hit was a working class Maori family, the Hunters of Riverton. Of the five Hunter boys who went to war only one returned. Joseph and David were both killed at Gallipoli in August 1915. Harry Hunter was killed in France in December 1917; his brother William in October 1918, the same month as Reg Christophers. John returned to New Zealand badly wounded after being awarded the Military Medal, along with his brother William, for bravery under fire.

Altogether, 62 New Zealand families lost three or four of their members in World War I. Seven sets of brothers from Southland Boys' High School alone never came home—the Baxters, Charlestons, Christophers, Gilmours, Hewats, Mathesons and McKenzies. From a school roll of under 200 in 1914, 17 former pupils were killed at Gallipoli and 110 for the whole war. Fifteen of them were university graduates, 26 held officer rank, including two of the Christophers boys. A small consolation to the Christophers family was that all of its sons had known graves. Thousands of other New Zealand soldiers did not, their epitaph only "Known Unto God. A Soldier of the Great War".

Just who were these four young men from what was in 1914 a small New Zealand town? What was it in their generation that they thought, felt and knew? Why and for what did they choose to fight?

Of the four brothers, Vic is perhaps the best known. He was both academically gifted and an outstanding sportsman, a quiet and unassuming young man with a wide circle of friends. Idealistic and thoughtful by nature, Vic wrote before the war to a magazine called *The Triad:* 'I think the only true and lasting morality must be based on what is natural, ever remembering that man has a divine nature as well as an animal one. The churches seem to have missed the essential teaching of the religion of their founder. Whatever the wonderful Nazarene was, one thing is clear, he was the prophet of the divine nature in man. He saw right into the depths of a man's soul… Evil cramps and destroys the growth of a man's soul. Good enables a man's soul and makes it richer and more beautiful.'

Vic's three brothers emerge as men driven by a strong sense of duty to King and country, natural leaders and widely respected by their brothers in arms. "Captain Christophers had turned up trumps, and was worth a tremendous lot to us," wrote fellow officer Captain Wilkes on the death of Herb just months before the Third Battle of the Somme. "He was a fine fellow and well liked by all the men," wrote rifleman Timpany. "I can assure you that he will be greatly missed."

Julian emerges from his letters to family as morally upright, patriotic and a good front-line soldier. On his death, Lieutenant Colonel Oliver Reid wrote to a relative: "It was very sad about poor old Christophers wasn't it? I have met several of his platoon mates, and they all speak very highly of him. They say he was always 'one of the boys', always did his full share and more of whatever required doing, and to cap it all kept straight—never drank or did any of the things soldiers do."

From his brief time at the front, Reg is remembered as a capable front-line officer dedicated to the welfare of his men, thorough in the performance of his duties and a strict disciplinarian. He tempered this, according to the American Society of Civil Engineers, with absolute fairness and impartiality. "He was one who, holding the highest ideals, lived up to them nobly, setting an example which anyone might do well to emulate, and finally giving his life in the finest way possible, in defence of his King and country."

The four Christophers boys all volunteered for service overseas in World War I, so why did they join up—in three cases clearly putting duty before family? Thousands of fellow New Zealanders had enlisted for patriotic reasons, to prove their courage in battle, or simply for adventure and the love of a fight. The brothers, however, were not impetuous youths but mature men in their late 20s and 30s, and three were married, two with children. By late 1916, the last two to enlist, Julian and his brother Reg, were well aware of the cost of the conflict in dead and broken men, many of whom would have been friends or former schoolmates. Significantly, they had seen two or more of their siblings killed in action and knew they had an equal chance of not surviving the war.

Arguably, the four brothers felt they had little choice but to go and fight. Exposed from an early age to the all-encompassing influence of schools, churches, Boy Scouts, school cadets, the Press and "imperialist" politicians, they and their generation had effectively been groomed for war. The process had begun well before the turn of the century, and focused at first on reshaping the behaviour and values of the nation's youth. "The footloose pub culture of the frontier," wrote historian Jock Phillips, "was to be replaced with a code of behaviour based on loyalty, honour, duty, self-discipline and self-sacrifice."[24]

At school, the young learned of the deeds of British military heroes and explorers—Drake and Raleigh, Hawkins, Frobisher and Cook, Wellington and Lord Nelson. They recited the poetry of Tennyson and Robert Bridges, and the ballads of Rudyard Kipling. They read G.A. Henty and Sir Henry Rider Haggard, and the medieval romances of William Morris. They read of heroic imperial adventures in South Africa dating back to the Zulu wars of 1879—at Isandlwana, Rorke's Drift, and Majuba Hill. Empire Day each year indoctrinated them in the superiority of the British race and loyalty to the empire. They were taught that war and the defence of empire was the ultimate test of their masculinity and that anyone not prepared to fight was not a real man.

Pro-empire organisations such as the Imperial Service League, the Boy Scouts, the National Defence League, the Victoria League, the Navy League, and the Legion of Frontiersmen sprang up around the country. Newspaper advertisements linked crockery, cigarettes, bicycles, chewing gum, boot polish and other consumer goods with imperialistic imagery and slogans. The widely read *Illustrated London News* and *Boys' Own* publications featured "ripping yarns of plucky young British lads."

Social Darwinist ideas prevalent at the time, mostly among the educated classes, added to the pressures on New Zealand's youth. Conflict, the argument ran, was a natural process by which fitter nations, races or individuals triumphed over weaker ones. Seduced by a culture of increasing materialism, moneymaking and pleasure seeking, the nation was becoming physically and morally flabby. Training for war, which fostered physical fitness, self-discipline and a sense of duty in the young, was an antidote to the "decadence" of modern society. War itself would reinvigorate the race and make it strong.

The pressures on young men to join up, however, came from a range of other sources—churches, newspaper editors, civic leaders and other authority figures, and even their families. Ormond Burton, soldier and leading post-war pacifist, recalled that his call to arms came in the form of the voices of those he knew and respected most. "Politicians and newspaper editors were then trusted by innocent young men like myself... What counted for me most was the fact that the Church, every part of her, backed the war as a great act of Christian righteousness."[25]

The churches, both before the war and during it, proved to be a particularly powerful agent of indoctrination. From the beginning, all the main denominations—Anglicans, Presbyterians, Methodists and Catholics—uncritically and effectively sanctified the Allied cause. For Catholic Archbishop Redwood the issue facing Britain and its empire was "whether militarism, despotism, and the barbarian"[26] were to triumph over civilisation. The Methodist conference of 1915 agreed, expressing the hope that God would "defend the right and cause the grinding militarism of Germany to cease from the earth."[27] Against these forces, and in spite of its defects, the conference decided, stood the British Empire—"the largest instalment of the Kingdom of God that has arisen among men."[28]

The director of Knox Theological College in Dunedin had no doubts about the righteousness of the cause, assuring his students that "the God of Battles will tread down our enemies." Those of his students who had enlisted were told that they were "following the path of Christian duty." Another churchman was more direct. "Christ's way," he told his flock, "led straight to the firing line and into the bayonet charge."[29] Everywhere, clergymen glorified serving soldiers as the "flower" of the nation's manhood, fighting in a righteous cause.[30]

As conflict wore on and the casualties grew, so too did the need to give meaning and a higher purpose to its huge sacrifices and loss of life. Here again the churches played a key role, assuring congregations that by their sacrifice, the nation's soldiers had earned an eternal reward. At the first Anzac Day service, Bishop Averill told his flock: "The brave men who will not come back to us have not finished their life of devotion, but have gone into God's higher training camp of service, where he has special work for each of them... As soldiers they will stand before the great white throne of God."[31]

Ormond Burton was scathing about these efforts to sanctify duty, sacrifice, and death in battle. "The greatest debacle of the war was without question that of the Christian Church," he wrote in later years. "She was subservient everywhere to national governments. All over the world Christian ministers closed their New Testaments, preached more paganism, and became the recruiting sergeants of the armies." Ironically, the clergymen so willing to commit young men to death or wounds on the battlefield were themselves exempt from compulsory military service.

From the outset, the nation's newspapers played a critical role in shaping mass perceptions of the war and mobilising support for it. Politically, they were a mix, but in 1914 they were united in supporting New Zealand's involvement. Thereafter most of them actively supported government decisions, aided patriotic fundraising, and demonised "shirkers,"conscientious objectors and others who questioned the war. Anti-German material was prominently featured and reports of German setbacks and atrocities were regularly published. It was a process, wrote social historian Steven Loveridge, that "tightened archetypes, eroded ambiguity, and suppressed alternatives." [32]

The *Poverty Bay Herald* was typical: "Victory will not be won without much self-sacrifice and suffering, but we feel that every loyal British subject will give this cheerfully in defence of all that is vital to his hearth and home. It is gratifying to know that New Zealand is doing its part speedily to assist the Empire." The trade union-leaning *Grey River Argus* warned: "Germany will find that she not only has to face England, for the whole of the Empire is standing alert and watchful, like a grim old lioness with her cubs."[33]

An Auckland newspaper asked its readers to imagine "Queen St, Ponsonby Rd, Khyber Pass and every street that guns can reach carpeted by slaughtered innocents! Hamilton as Louvain; Takapuna as Liege; Whangarei and the furthest farms given up to "frightfulness!" Defeat, it was argued, would see local security collapse. "German officers would swagger in the streets of Auckland and New Zealand. Women would be treated as Belgian women have been treated."[34]

In this way the country's most influential newspapers became agents of the State for the duration of the war, abandoning their traditional role as critics of government actions and policies—"speaking truth to power."

Exceptions were the *Maoriland Worker* and the tabloid *New Zealand Truth*, both of which were critical of New Zealand's involvement in the war, the latter seeing it as a war to benefit the capitalist class at the expense of the nation's workers.

Censorship also played its part in supporting State versions of the conduct of the war. This ensured that New Zealand families had minimal information about where their soldier sons, brothers and husbands were deployed, the conditions under which they were fighting, and the casualties their units had suffered. Soldiers' letters home were invariably censored, along with cables from the front sent via the United Press agency. These were censored not only in the field but in London, then again in Australia before being passed on to New Zealand and censored a fourth time.

Helping to conceal the truth was the British tendency to describe their military campaigns—past and present—in grandiose, heroic terms. "Retreat or advance, win or lose, blunder or bravery, murderous folly or unyielding resolution, all emerge alike clothed in dignity and touched with glory," wrote historian Barbara Tuchman. "Everyone is splendid, soldiers are staunch, commanders cool, the fighting magnificent… Mistakes, failures, stupidities or other causes of disaster mysteriously vanish. Disasters are recorded with care and pride and become transmuted into things of beauty."[35]

Inevitably, the education system, the churches, the newspapers and other powerful agents of indoctrination would have influenced the decisions of the Christophers boys to enlist. Two of them, Vic and Herb, did so immediately on the outbreak of war. The other two brothers may also have attempted to join up but been temporarily rejected because the recruiters at the time favoured single men with no family or other encumbrances. At this time, both Julian and Reg were married with children and holding down responsible jobs—Julian as a manager for a stock and station firm and Reg as a civil engineer working for a North Island county council.

After the deaths of their brothers in the first and second years of the war, both knew that they had a good chance of being killed or seriously wounded if they enlisted. In the end, the demand for reinforcements caught them up and both responded to the call of duty over that of family. As Julian wrote in June 1916: "My knee seems better, and if strong enough, it is my turn to go next, and I intend to go." In fact, he was unfit for active service and the army should have rejected him out of hand.

8

THE REASON WHY

*"The First World War is a mystery. Its origins are mysterious.
So is its course. Why did a prosperous continent, at the height of
its success as a source and agent of global wealth and power and
at one of the peaks of its intellectual and cultural achievements,
choose to risk all it had won for itself and all it had offered to the
world in the lottery of a vicious and local internecine conflict? The
conflict could have been brought to a quick and decisive conclusion
within months of its outbreak, but the combatants opted instead to
mobilise for total war and commit their young manhood to mutual
and essentially pointless slaughter."*

— British military historian John Keegan,
The First World War

So was it all for nothing, a futile waste of lives in a war fought to protect interests that were not our own? What did four brothers from a provincial New Zealand town believe so strongly that it sent them 20,000 kilometres from home to fight and die for Britain and its empire?

Like the majority of New Zealanders, the Christophers boys believed what the country's politicians, reinforced by its newspapers, had told them in the years before the war—that German imperial ambitions were a serious threat not only to Britain and its empire but to the security and prosperity of New Zealand as part of the empire. Early on, the newspapers had brought them reports of Germany's naval build-up, in itself a grave threat to British security. Then in 1914 came news of its invasion of Belgium and the atrocities committed against that country's civilian population. Most now believed Germany under its Kaiser to be an aggressive, militaristic nation aiming at world domination and that this threat had to be met.

Twentieth century scholarship suggests that they had good grounds for thinking so. Professor Fritz Fischer, described as the most important German historian of the 20th century, argued that his country deliberately instigated World War I in an attempt to destroy the growing economic and military power of Russia, dominate Europe and become a world power in its own right. Professor Jürgen Tampke, another German academic now living in Australia, has gone further to claim that Germany's expansion plans extended deep into the South Pacific to include both Australia and New Zealand.[36]

The Massey administration that governed New Zealand during the war years had no doubts that the nation's security and economic well-being were bound up with the fate of Britain and its empire. New Zealand was reliant on the British market for 80 per cent of its exports, which made the protection of that market and the trade routes that fed it of vital national concern. To the north, a new Asian power, Japan, had emerged after its victory in the Russo-Japanese War of 1904–05 and was now the strongest naval power in the Pacific region.

The collapse of British naval power as a result of a victory by the German High Seas Fleet over the British Grand Fleet, the policymakers reasoned, would leave Australia and New Zealand exposed not only to raids on their ports and shipping but to the territorial ambitions of Germany, and possibly Japan, in the South Pacific. A post-war settlement with a defeated Britain might see New Zealand lose its sovereignty altogether and become part of the German Empire.

An unwritten alliance, known as "imperial defence," had been in place from the 1880s and to ensure that it remained so the Massey Government was more than willing to send troops to stand by the mother country on the battlefields of Europe. In this, it was supported by the great majority of New Zealanders for the duration of the war, including those who fought at the front.

"In spite of the carnage, there were no calls to bring the troops home, no riots or other civil unrest, no revolutions or uprisings as were occurring in Russia and Germany," noted Steven Loveridge. "Even in 1917–18 when all ideas of 'the great adventure' had dissipated and conscription introduced, 26,000 men still volunteered."[37] For every one conscript over the course of the war, three men would volunteer for active service, including all four of the Christophers brothers. In a broader sense, it was a mark of the ability of a modern state—through education and coercion—to mobilise almost an entire population for the purposes of war.

What made these men willing to fight and kept them loyal to the cause over four years of immense suffering and loss? Patriotism, along with a sense of duty instilled by the churches and the education system, played a key role, as did a pervasive "culture of sacrifice" that became stronger as the war progressed. What gave them and their families reason to endure was the hope that when the conflict was finally over the foundations of a better world would be laid. "Nothing less," wrote Barbara Tuchman, "could give dignity or sense to monstrous offensives in which thousands and hundreds of thousands were killed to gain ten yards and exchange one wet-bottomed trench for another."[38]

It proved a false hope. Twenty years on, Germany would rise again to threaten the peace of Europe. Once again, a new generation of New Zealanders, and a new expeditionary force, would go to the defence of Britain and its empire, and again their country would pay a heavy price in the blood of its youth.

9

COUNTING THE COST

Almost a generation of the best young men were wiped out, and throughout my life I have been conscious of this deprivation. In all walks of life many of those who would have been the leaders were missing. The ineptitudes of the decades between the two wars, both in Europe and New Zealand, may in large measure be due to this. Not only these men, but those who would have been their children are missing, and we have had to do our best without them. It is hard to estimate what human loss and depreciation was the result of these experiences.

– Sir Douglas Robb, an undergraduate of
Auckland University in 1917, and later its Chancellor

The first and greatest loss to New Zealand from World War I was people. From a population of just under 1,100,000 in 1914 just over 100,000 served overseas in the New Zealand Expeditionary Force. Only Britain mobilised a higher number of troops as a percentage of population—11.2 per cent compared to New Zealand's 8.9 perc ent and Australia's 6.8 per cent.

Of these, 18,500 would die of wounds or disease on the battlefields of Gallipoli, Palestine, and Europe, and over 40,000 would be wounded. Among them were those who would have been the leaders of the post-war generation, its politicians and top administrators; its skilled farmers, businessmen, tradesmen and professional men; its nation-defining writers, journalists and academics.

Ten years later young men were still dying as a direct result of wounds or sickness suffered during the war. Mental illness blighted the lives of thousands more, and suicides were common. These were the victims of what came to be known as Post Traumatic Stress Syndrome (PTSD)—the result of combat fatigue or exhaustion caused by prolonged exposure to foul weather, lack of sleep, and the constant threat of death by shellfire, gas, bomb or bullet. They were the silent men who in many cases were unable to admit or confront their distress, who had seen too much of the brutality of war and seen it too young.

As Pugsley wrote: "It was a terrible price exacted from a small country isolated from the events of an essentially European conflagration."[39] "The war affected all levels of New Zealand society like no other tragedy," observed another military historian. "By the Battle of Passchendaele in 1917, scarcely a family had been left untouched by the death or injury of someone dear to them."[40]

Loss of human capital apart, the war was expensive, doubling government debt and resulting in a 60 per cent rise in expenditure over its four-year course. Over 80 million pounds were borrowed to cover war expenses, two-thirds of it from the populace in the form of low-interest war bonds. Taxes and duties were imposed on many goods, imports and services as a means of gathering extra revenue. Consumption of key resources like coal and petrol were restricted because of their importance to New Zealand's industry and transport systems.

The cost of living rose by nearly 40 per cent between 1914 and 1918 in spite of the efforts of a Board of Trade to set maximum prices for essential food items, hold down rents and mortgage rates, and investigate charges of war profiteering. The economic damage went deeper as the demand for manpower drained the country of labour, skills and capital needed by the farming, mining, manufacturing and service industries. The weapons, clothing and footwear industries prospered because they directly served the war effort, but other manufacturing was hard hit. The rundown of social services and public works over the war years inevitably affected health care, education and other services.

The war also divided communities and restricted democratic freedoms, if only temporarily. Censorship controlled the access of citizens to information about the progress of the war; conscription, introduced in 1916, forced thousands of young men into the army, many of them against their will. Citizens of enemy countries living in New Zealand, and even naturalised New Zealanders with German names, were classified as enemy aliens. These could be imprisoned on suspicion of spying, undermining the war effort, or inciting resistance of any kind. Internment camps were set up and some 500 aliens—mostly citizens of German or Austrian nationality—were imprisoned in them during the war.[41]

Freedom of information was a major casualty of the war, and by deliberate policy of all Allied governments. Journalists' reports back to New Zealand from the front were heavily censored, first on the battlefield, then by military censors in London, again in Australia, and finally by the defence ministry in Wellington. The flow of other information in and out of New Zealand was strictly controlled. The reasons were clear enough—a fear that militarily important information could be passed to the enemy and that public morale would be affected if news of military setbacks was published too quickly or without a degree of positive spin.

Control of information began early. The first reports of the Gallipoli landing heard by the citizenry of New Zealand contained no word of the military debacle it in fact was. Instead, a telegram sent by the British Government spoke of the "splendid gallantry" of the New Zealand troops and praised them for their "magnificent achievement." News of the landings on 25 April and the nearly1000 New Zealanders killed did not reach the country until six weeks later. Nor were the soldiers at the front better informed, with many complaining that they knew nothing about how the war was progressing.

Most newspapers accepted a certain level of censorship; what rankled was the degree of control. "It is not enough," wrote the editor of the *Feilding Star* "that the news is censored in London and Australia before it reaches us, but yet another board of censors must sieve it in New Zealand."[42] The *Southland Times* agreed, protesting at the way State censors managed the flow of information about the progress of the war. "The war," the newspaper said, "could be called the 'Silent War,'"[43] and it called for the official war correspondent to be sacked. A Greymouth editor complained: "What we want is the truth or nothing at all. From the beginning to end we have been fed with vagaries and lies."[44]

In April 1916, the censorship regulations were tightened to forbid any mention of a soldier's unit, summaries of casualties, and the publication of uncensored soldiers' letters. A charge of sedition for criticising conscription and the military itself was written into legislation. Militant left-wing groups which threatened to destabilise the war effort by opposing conscription and supporting strikes were closely watched.

Specific books and journals were banned and the Minister of Defence was given power to censor or ban any films about the war which would make men less keen to enlist. Citizens could be stopped from writing, publishing or selling a range of political, philosophical, social or religious books or even talking freely. Socialist and pacifist works were kept out of the country, along with any literary works that might threaten the status quo.[45] The irony was that the State, while claiming to be fighting for freedom, kept tightening its grip on an essential component of that freedom.

Conscription, introduced in August 1916 as the demand for men grew and the number of volunteers fell, was another major constraint on individual freedom. Each recruiting district was assigned a quota to be met by volunteers, or by balloted conscripts if the numbers required by the army fell short. Two divisions of recruits were established—a first division of all men aged 20–46 who were single, widowers without children or married after 1 May 1915, and a second division of predominantly married men. The first division was to be exhausted before men from the second were called upon, and it was under this category that Reg and Julian Christophers, as married men, enlisted.

Just under 135,000 men were balloted for overseas service and between a third and a half applied for exemption over the two years conscription was in force. Grounds for the applications included health, impending marriage, business reasons or employment in an essential industry, and religious and conscientious objections. Each appeal was heard by a Military Appeal Board, which either allowed it, dismissed it, or adjourned it indefinitely.

The main opposition to conscription came from those who objected on religious grounds, socialists, Irish and Maori. Socialists argued that conscription served capitalist interests rather than those of the working class. Irish objectors were unwilling to fight for a Britain they saw as their historical oppressor. Maori whose tribes had suffered badly as a result of the land wars of the 1860s objected to fighting in a "Pakeha" war.

For its part, the United Federation of Labour claimed conscription would make the working class "fight the battles of the Empire, foot the bills and rob them of the freedom which they consider they are fighting (for) and paying to uphold." The newly formed Labour Party opposed conscription as "the negation of liberty" and the fight against it a fight against "militarism and capitalism." The State, it argued, must field nothing but a voluntary citizen army.[46]

As the demand for fighting men grew, the pressures to enlist intensified. Newspapers and cartoonists made a particular target of so-called "shirkers" and conscientious objectors. Women in Auckland and Christchurch handed out white feathers denoting cowardice to young men they thought were avoiding service at the front. Champion tennis player Anthony Wilding commented at the time: "I verily believe that it would take a braver man to stand down than become a soldier."[47]

Returned men faced a different set of problems. "The men who had marched off to the cheers of an admiring and supportive public returned to an unsympathetic and uncaring society, and a government which showed little interest in the plight of men who had been seriously wounded," wrote Phillips, Boyack and Malone. "While the public gave its ready support to the erection of expensive monuments to the dead, those who returned quickly became the forgotten victims of the war."[48]

The Government, however, did not neglect their dependents, particularly those who would have struggled to make ends meet if the family breadwinner was serving overseas. The wives and children of soldiers were eligible for war pensions, along with elderly people who depended financially on sons serving at the front. From 1916, trustees could be appointed to manage a soldier's farm or business where their families were struggling to keep it running. From 1917, families of men on active service were eligible for help with paying rent, taxes, insurance premiums and other business expenses.[49]

Although there was no civilian conscription as such, a National Efficiency Board set guidelines for which categories of men should be kept at home to keep the country running, and established methods of maximising industrial efficiency. Men rejected for military service, women, schoolboys and retirees were encouraged to work in essential industries like agricultural production, food processing and transport.

If World War I proved socially and economically disruptive, it also brought thousands of women out of the home and into the workforce. Women served at the front as doctors, nurses and nurse aides, truck and ambulance drivers—over 600 of them in the New Zealand Army Nursing Service alone. In government departments, banks, insurance companies and in other white-collar occupations, they took the place of men who were serving overseas.[50]

On the large farms and estates, they deserted menial domestic work for better-paid jobs in shops and factories. Thousands more did farm work for no wages at all in the milking sheds, stockyards, and paddocks of small family farms across the country. Middle class women worked alongside working class women as chauffeurs, orderlies, cooks, and general workers of all kinds.

Unsurprisingly, they faced opposition from ultra-conservatives who saw working women as abandoning traditional roles as wives and mothers and their duty "to embody and maintain social standards." They would encounter prejudice from those who saw women in the workforce as a threat to the traditional masculine role of family breadwinner. They would face resistance from trade unions that had won liveable wages and conditions for skilled men over the years and were fearful that women would now be employed on lower pay. Almost everywhere, however, women put paid to old assumptions that they were unsuited to particular occupations for lack of physical strength, endurance, or intellectual ability.

Significantly, the war had a major impact on the country's development constitutionally and status internationally. Its political leaders, Massey and Ward, attended imperial conferences in London to discuss the progress of the war, then took part in the Versailles Peace Conference that formally ended it. As a member of the League of Nations that emerged from the peace settlement, New Zealand took its first step on the road to independence.

10

THE PITY OF WAR

For by my glee might many men have laughed,
And of my weeping something had been left,
Which must die now. I mean the truth untold,
The pity of war, the pity war distilled.
                    – World War I soldier-poet Wilfred Owen

I n September 1917, Quintin, the youngest of the five Christophers brothers, was ordered to report for military service at an Invercargill recruitment
centre. In the manner of the time, the tone of the summons was bleak: "If
you fail to parade as ordered above you are liable to be arrested forthwith by
the Civil Police, and, on conviction, to be punished as a deserter." Quintin
was not to answer the call. After an approach to the Military Appeal Board
he was exempted from overseas service, most likely on family care grounds.

His three older brothers had taken the harder road, enlisting despite
the deaths of siblings, the demands of family life and the risk that they too
would be killed or seriously wounded. What drove them, it seems clear
from their letters, was not a desire to revenge the deaths of siblings but a set
of widely shared social values quite alien to modern generations—loyalty
to King and country, a sense of duty to their brothers and others who had
paid the ultimate price, and a willingness to sacrifice themselves for a cause
they saw as greater than them all. In this sense they were men of their time.

Before volunteering for active service, Reg wrote to his aunt: "What
an awful thing it would be for all the noble lives that have fallen that we,
the living, did not see the thing through to the bitter end!" Just before he
enlisted, his brother Julian told Quintin: "I do not like breaking up my
happy home, but every sacrifice has to be made these days."

While they lived, the four brothers endured in full the trials of life at the front: relentless heat, flies and disease at Gallipoli, hunger and thirst, the stink of corpses left unburied out in No Man's Land; the howling of "Allah!" in the night as waves of Turkish troops flung themselves against the Anzac defences; biscuit-box crosses marking the graves of mates who now lay forever in Gallipoli's hard clay.

On the Western Front, they had faced an enemy at the end of a bayonet during major offensives, but otherwise rarely seen except on night patrols and trench raids. They had endured the misery of trench life with its rain, cold, mud and endless hard labour; the fear of death always from shellfire, mortars, rifle and machine-gun fire, or gas; the constant need for food, warmth and sleep. "Nothing," wrote military historian John Terraine, "was more corrosive of the human spirit than trench warfare, whose main components were ever-present danger, fatigue, squalor, and inertia."[51]

Two of the brothers—Julian and Reg—had "gone over the top" in attacks on heavily defended enemy positions, advancing across terrain typically deep in mud and cratered by artillery fire. "If made through a heavy barrage and under machine-gun fire," wrote Ormond Burton, "it was test of cold nerve."[52]

In the close confines of the trenches, they and their mates had forged bonds that would survive them and the war itself. "The individual soldier's world, and all that really mattered to him, was his section or at the most his platoon," wrote Richard Holmes. "They lived together, fought together, shared their food and drink, and wrote to the relatives of the men who were killed."[53] Their lives were always on the line and they knew it.

Had they lived, the Christophers brothers would have returned to a country much changed by four years of war and seemingly determined to erase all memories of the horror its soldiers had endured. As at the end of the New Zealand Wars of the 1860s, there appeared to have been an unconscious need to "suppress the pain and play down the unacceptable." Instead, the Great War came to be commemorated as "a proud assertion of New Zealand nationality, the proof of our superior manhood. The dead were presented as an inspiration rather than a warning."[54]

As veterans, the brothers would have adapted gradually to their return to civilian life, wanting only to forget and move on. But if seriously wounded or mentally damaged, they would have struggled to find their feet. Wounded Gallipoli veterans found themselves "strangers in the prosperous land they now called 'Home'", wrote Pugsley. "There was plenty of work for those prepared to get stuck in, but they could not. They were hospitalised or required continuing outpatient care. The years of prosperity into the 1920s became for them years of recovery from wounds or the after-effects of dysentery and disease."[55]

Attitudes to war would also have undergone a major shift. "The old certainties were now eroded or had vanished entirely—convictions that war reinvigorated nations, created character, was manly and glorious, and victory could be relatively bloodless," wrote historian Glyn Harper. "Notions of duty, honour, sacrifice and Empire also suffered. New Zealanders came to realise that they were different from the British and other nationalities and so a sense of identity was born."[56]

On the home front, their families had endured as best they could, waiting anxiously for news from the battlefield of sons, brothers, lovers and friends. After every major offensive involving the New Zealanders, local newspapers would publish long lists of casualties, obituaries of well-known local boys, and soldiers' letters that became increasingly graphic as the war wore on. Feared above all was the telegraph boy's knock on the door announcing the death of a family member at the front.

How Anthony and Juliet coped with the deaths of their sons in the years after the war is unknown, but for most parents the loss of a son in battle was the cruellest blow, condemning many to lifelong anger and depression. A woman who lost two brothers in France wrote 70 years later: "My mother had her photo taken after her family losses. She was 41, and the photo reveals precisely how she was then… haunted, bereft."[57]

Anthony, who had embarked for New Zealand and a new life over 50 years before, had lived to see his family almost destroyed by war. After it, according to a family source, he squandered most of his assets playing cards (baccarat) at the Invercargill Club—an attempt perhaps to dull the pain of his loss. A hint that the family was struggling financially as a result appears in a letter Juliet wrote in later years asking that the names of her boys be inscribed on her gravestone. "I think I have saved enough money," she wrote, "I have 62 pounds in (the) Savings Bank."

Quintin's son John, a former deputy mayor of the Waikato town of Matamata, feels no bitterness about what befell his family, but admits to a certain pride in the sacrifices his uncles made during the Great War. In the family tradition, he himself stepped up for combat duty, volunteering for service as a pilot in World War II and seeing action as a gunner with the New Zealand forces in Korea in 1950.

That experience, however, left him with firm views on the need for well-trained and equipped military forces: "Six times in the 20th century New Zealand sent expeditionary forces overseas inadequately trained and grossly underarmed. Over 30,000 New Zealanders have been killed in action in these encounters because the need to maintain adequate combat forces was not considered a top priority."

Since 1927, the Christophers Memorial Shield has been competed for annually by students of Southland Boys' High School. It was given to the school by Juliet Christophers as a memorial to her four sons, all of whom had been prominent sportsmen at the school. For many years after the war, Juliet placed a wreath on behalf of the Returned Services Association (RSA) at Invercargill's Anzac Day service.

The school now marks every Anzac Day with a special ceremony in memory of the four Christophers boys. The music is Elgar's *Nimrod* from the *Enigma Variations* and *Jupiter* from *The Planets* by Gustav Holst. Versions of the National Anthem in English and Maori and a vigorous haka by the whole school complete the ceremony.

Close to the Gallipoli beach where the New Zealanders landed on 25 April is Vic Christophers' simple grave. "The waves break along the bay a little way from his feet," wrote his friend Ernie Royd. "The sun climbs over a clear sky above the tree that shades him and sets in front of his biscuit box cross every golden evening and birds fly over and flowers bloom… But also the rifles crack and the big guns roar and the bombs thud and he takes little heed of that so maybe he's as well off."

Time has worked its changes on the battlefields of France and Belgium where Vic's three brothers and 12,500 other New Zealand soldiers now lie. "The battlefields today are green and gold again," wrote Major General Sir Ernest Swinton just twenty years after the guns fell silent. "Young trees are everywhere and the desolate waste of shell hole and mud has given way to pasture land and waving corn. Proudly on the heights stand the memorials to the fallen, and in the valleys and on hillside peacefully lie the silent cities where they rest." Brothers in arms forever now, soldiers of the Great War.

Bound for the front. 2nd Lieutenant Reginald Christophers (fourth from right at back) with fellow officers and nurses of the 34th Reinforcements aboard the troopship Remuera in June 1918.

Christophers family archive

New Zealand Division commander Major General Sir Andrew Russell inspects troops of the Otago Battalion before they go into action on the Western Front. RSA Collection.

Alexander Turnbull Library

Anzac snipers at work during the Gallipoli campaign. RSA Collection.

Alexander Turnbull Library

"Diggers" at rest in freshly dug trenches during the great German offensive of March 1918.

RSA Collection. Alexander Turnbull Library

Spoils of war. German machine guns and artillery captured by the New Zealanders at Messines on display in the French town of Bailleul.

RSA Collection. Alexander Turnbull Library

New Zealand troops march through Bailleul en route to the front.

Alexander Turnbull Library

LETTERS FROM THE FRONT

These letters are from soldiers from the Otago and Southland provinces who served in the same units as the Christophers brothers at Gallipoli and later on the Western Front. From a training camp in New Zealand to the landing at Gallipoli, to the disaster at Passchendaele, they provide a vivid picture of life as it was for the ordinary New Zealand soldier in World War I.

Thomas Gibson Denniston
Otago Infantry Battalion

Tauherenikau Camp, 28 December 1915
Dear Mother
The day we arrived here it was blowing a gale, and everybody's first impression of the place was unfavourable. However, matters improved and we began to like the place, when the tucker took a turn for the worse. We had been warned by a mounted man that it would get less and worse gradually until we squealed. At last the limit was reached when we got a dish of dishwater and three pieces of fatty meat for 8 men and tea full of dust and ashes. Then crawlers in the cheese and meat etc. Everybody simultaneously, as the expression is, "went maggoty," with the result that the doctor condemned the meat,

the cookhouses and the whole shebang. It was not the cooks' fault. They admitted to us that they lifted the bugs off the top of the stew with a ladle as they rose to the surface. This is our first day in camp since the Xmas holidays and things are only middling, but will have to improve again tomorrow or there will be another roar.

Then the Xmas leave arrangements have been causing trouble. This time the fault of the railway dept. It was the holiday crowds and the race-trains first and Tommy A. (the soldiers) last. They said they could only take 500 into Wellington each day. Those 500 had to be drawn out of a hat. What a squeal there was! Eventually the majority of the remainder got leave on Friday to return at 4.20 on Monday. On the station on Monday was "No soldiers allowed on board." About 50 jumped the train and officials tried to eject them. Failing that they threatened to hold the train. "Then your **** train can stop here, for we're not getting off." Eventually they travelled by it. The remainder travelled by the 10.10pm train and got to camp about 3am, a rotten journey and a 4 or 5-mile tramp at the end of it.

At present it is raining like fun and the huts are rotten old things and leak plentifully. Another rotten trick. We don't mind rough living and rough tucker—when unavoidable. "Come, be a hero and fight for your country." All right. "Now we've got you, live like a pig and be d—d to you." But it is no good wandering on like this. The work is not hard yet—I think only getting more interesting—bayonet fighting, night operations etc. I know the writing is rotten but am writing on a broken upturned box with 2 inches of candle stuck into it. Still raining…

Tom Denniston wrote again to his mother on 2 October 1916. He was now in First London General Hospital with a bullet wound through the chest after taking part in the New Zealand Division's attack in the Third Battle of the Somme two weeks before.

Victor James Christophers
Otago Mounted Rifles

4 May 1915

Just before he sailed for Gallipoli, Vic wrote his parents a last
letter from Egypt: "You will no doubt read full accounts of the
landing at the Dardanelles in the newspapers, but I will tell you
all I have heard about it. I cannot vouch for the accuracy of
what I write, but they are just tales told by the wounded who
have returned after waiting about in the transport for two or
three weeks.

Our fellows made a landing on Sunday the 25th April. The
Allies landed on six different beaches. The Australians and New
Zealanders landed at a place called Saribair. Steep slopes arise
from the beach and scrub about two feet high covers the slopes.
All seemed quiet until the landing parties neared the shore,
but when they got within a few chains of the beach, concealed
batteries, machine guns and riflemen opened a deadly fire…
Some boats were sunk before they reached the beach and to
add to the difficulty of landing, barbed wire entanglements
were found under the water.

Casualties were heavy. Some Australian companies were
nearly wiped out but boatloads rushed ashore and the colonials
scrambled up the slopes and went for the Turks with their
bayonets. Excitement was intense. I believe stokers who were
watching the fight from one transport jumped overboard,
picked up bayonets and joined the melee. Some of the boat
crews who left their boats on the beach joined in the fun.

The warships opened fire. The *Queen Elizabeth*, or "Lizzie"
as the fellows call her, the largest and latest warship in the
navy, did especially good work. Her shots are deafening and
are deadly effective. The Turkish batteries are concealed in the
scrub and it was difficult to pick them up. Landing parties
located these and signalled the ranges to the warships. Some
Turkish warships attempted to join the fight but whenever they
caught sight of Lizzie they immediately made them themselves
scarce.

The Turks would not stand up to the bayonet and all who could run fled as soon as the colonials reached the trenches. The Turks did a lot of damage with sharpshooters, who were hidden in the scrub. Many wore khaki similar to our uniforms and it was often difficult to pick enemies from friends. The Turks are mostly led by German officers. In the meantime, landings had been made on the beaches by English troops, while French troops landed on the Asiatic side. The Allies have now secured a strong position on the Gallipoli Peninsula and we are waiting to hear of further developments.

Some of our men were too eager and chased the enemy too far and came right up against the enemy's guns and were forced to retire with heavy losses. The Otago-Southland men suffered least of all. Their OC (commanding officer) Colonel Moore entrenched his men as soon as he got them in a good position and this is what the others should have done.

Every day ships are arriving here with wounded. Fellows treat a wound through the arm or leg very lightly. It is surprising how quickly a wound heals. Many who returned here last week wounded are on their way back to the front. The Navy are very enthusiastic over the achievements of the Army and the soldiers' chief amusement is to watch the warships bombarding. Hope the censors pass this.

James Gardner Jackson
Stretcher-bearer, New Zealand Field Ambulance

Anzac Cove, Gallipoli, 11 June 1915
My Dear Father, Mother, Jean and all at home,
The censorship is very strict here and we can write very little of the real things that are going on. Your own officer first censors it then the colonel might have a look at it and after these two the censor goes through it again. I notice in the papers that some very funny mistakes are made in the war news. The papers say that we have occupied Maidos. Well if you look at a good map of Gallipoli you will easily see that if that were the case there would be very little need for much more fighting.

Maidos is above the Narrows, past Chanak and Kilid Bahr, and it is the Narrows that we are after. Maidos is about 6 miles west of us and over the most difficult fighting ground imaginable. Just a series of steep ridges with clay faces, and where trees can grow the land is covered with a thick, prickly bush about 5 ft high. Ideal ground for snipers and they make good use of it whenever they can.

Our front is 2 and a half to 5 miles long, counting outposts, and at no place are we more than three-quarters of a mile from the sea. On this area of ground we have about 30,000 Australians and New Zealanders, and you can see that there is a lot of crowding in places. We have established a good footing on the top of the surrounding hills and have improved our position by building roads and saps which protect us from shell fire a good bit. But one can never say where a shell will burst and we still have a good few wounded from that cause. Our own company has lost up to date 16 wounded and 5 killed.

The first week was the hardest that we have had so far and I hope for a long time yet. We landed early in the afternoon of the first Sunday at a little bay called by us Anzac Cove. It is about 300 yds long between the two points and on the north is a fine big bay perhaps five miles around to a point called Cape Suvla. To the south is a point 2 miles away called Gaba Tepe where the Turks had a fort and a battery of field artillery. Straight in front of the landing is a big hill about 300–400 ft high which rises very sharply from the sea and it was here that the Turks had a machine gun and were entrenched first at a little knoll 100 ft high and then on the main hill…

When we landed we were brought from the transport *Gosler*, a captured German boat, on the destroyer *Foxhound* to half a mile from the shore, from where we came in in a rowing boat half full of water and with about 30 men in it. It was the slowest yet most exciting row that I had ever been in. The shrapnel was trying to stop us all the time and it seemed hours before we ran ashore. This shrapnel is very deadly stuff if it catches anyone in an exposed position, and no position is more exposed than in an open rowboat out on the water. It was our first experience of it and I can tell you we did not like it. Only one in the boat was hit. We can hear it coming just like a rocket at a fireworks display, but of course we can't see it. It bursts with a deafening report and each shell scatters about 250 small pellets of lead with great force, enough to go right through a man. I am trying to get one of the shells with the time-fuse cap home with this letter if possible.

After reaching dry land we started work straight away. We did not have to look far for wounded who required attention. They were lying all about the beach and in the bushes and we gradually cleared the hillside until we reached the top about 8 o'clock in the evening. Then the trench work started and it was real hard... It rained early in the morning and made the work very awkward and dangerous. It took us exactly 4 hours to bring one man from away in the back of somewhere. We had five warships doing great work with their big guns and they must have accounted for hundreds of Turks.

On the Tuesday we came around to the left flank and at 1.30 next morning we had brought down 105 men from the trenches, treated them and evacuated them along the beach to Anzac Cove. The distance to carry back one is one-and-a-half miles and not over paved roads. One night we went aboard a destroyer, the *Bulldog*, and were landed at Cape Helles to do some more work there. The infantry did some good fighting and we had some of the most risky work to do; that is, stretcher-bearing over level ground 400 yds from the firing line. There was nothing to stop the bullets that had missed their mark and it is a wonder that more of us did not get hit.

We rested here for 8 or 9 days and really enjoyed ourselves. There was plenty of water, a commodity which is very scarce around here at Anzac. The ration is half a gallon per man per day. Just try and see how far it goes for tea, washing up and everything it is needed for. We caught tortoises down at the cape and very handy things they are. You have to pounce on them before they can get up speed and then invent some way to kill them. The flesh makes lovely soup but best of all are the eggs. They make a good custard with ground-up biscuits and water…

The French down here are good fighters and their artillery is splendid. Their 175mm guns are perfect long-range guns and can do a lot of damage… The fighting is all trench work and in some places we live an underground life. These trenches at certain parts are not more than 15 yds apart and bombs are thrown pretty freely. I suppose the papers say that we are fighting great, but if you could see our position you would think that they could drive us off the top of the hill with one big rush. But the Turks have never learned the proper use of the bayonet yet, although we did give them a good lesson [on] the first day.

Henry Devenish Skinner
Otago Infantry Battalion

St David's Hospital, Malta, August 13 1915
Dear People,
I am going to give you my impression of three days and nights of fighting against the Turks. If I seem to dwell on the terrible, remember it is that which attracts one's attention and sticks in the memory. And nothing I can say will convey one thousandth part of the horror of the reality…

On the afternoon of Tuesday August 5th, Ellis and I sorted and packed our belongings and tidied the bivouac in Monash Valley, which had been more of a home to us than any other place in the nine weeks since we had landed. We ate whatever food we could not carry in our haversacks and I computed our respective chances for the ensuing action. I put them at 2 to 1 that one of us would be wounded and 3 to 1 against either being killed.

Night came, beautifully clear; rifle fire grew brisker and we marched off. I carried 220 rounds, my iron ration, a shirt, pair of socks, shaving gear and such extra food as I could cram into pockets and haversack. We marched down the winding sap past the shadowy water tanks to the beach, then north among the stacks of stores and ammunition into the sap again. On our left was the sea, on our right the group of hills, one slope of which we have held since the beginning, and the peak of which—Hill 971—we were to capture.

Towards dawn we were camped in a little valley full of scrub. We spent Friday hiding in the valley. Twice a German Taube flew over us but we lay still under the scrub and they did not see us. In the morning I went up with the water bottles of our section to the tanks on Walker's Ridge, a terrible climb in the heat. As we stood in a long queue the bullets began to drop about us aimed at some officers on the bank above us and Kelly, a corporal in D company, was struck and fell dead…

As we approached our outpost the rifle fire increased and bombs came from the hill on our right. The sap ended and we lay down on the flat at the foot of the hills. Two searchlights were playing from the destroyers off Suvla Bay. A Tommy regiment emerged from the sap and moved off in a confused way with much hoarse whispering and running to and fro, apparently deploying between us and the beach, and then moving north… Our work was now to advance up a long valley and to hold the shoulders of 971 by dawn. The mounteds were to sweep up the spur on our right and another detachment to do the same on our left.

We crept through a gap cut by our engineers in the barbed wire entanglement and stood confused in the dark amongst the stubble of a little field, spurs on either hand and the Turkish trench spitting fire at us less than 100 yards ahead. There was hesitation and various orders. We extended in an uneven line across the gully. Someone shouted "Charge!" and we rushed forward yelling…. McCaw got a bullet through the shoulder and there were others. A party of bomb throwers ran forward and took the second trench without opposition, which was a good thing because the bombs were a failure. Then came a wait. We had lost our platoon sergeant and no one took charge.

At last we moved off up a valley. On our right we could hear firing and an occasional cheer as our fellows charged a fresh trench…

The last page of this letter has been lost but it is clear that it describes the attack by the New Zealand Infantry Brigade on the heights of Chunuk Bair on 7 August 1915. The Otago Battalion led the night assault but the heights were ultimately taken and held for 72 hours by Lieutenant Colonel Malone's Wellington Battalion.

Leonard (Len) Mitchell Hart
Otago Infantry Battalion

January 1 1916

Dear Father, Mother and Connie,

Since last writing I have been transferred from Pont de Keubba hospital (Cairo) to the convalescent hospital Luxor, where I arrived about a fortnight ago. I am feeling much better now and am getting back to my old condition slowly but surely… If I remember rightly we left Alexandria on the fourth of August, arriving at Lemnos Island on Friday, the sixth. Besides ourselves, there were a large number of Australians and Tommies aboard, and the steamer (a large one) was loaded to her utmost. We were obliged to sleep on, and under, the mess tables, or, in fact, anywhere we could get.

At about 9pm we rounded the southernmost point of the [Gallipoli] peninsula where a heavy bombardment from the warships was in progress. The Turkish forts replied at intervals but their fire was not nearly so incessant as that of the warships. It was pitch-dark, and this made the flashes from the guns and the bursting of shells show up all the plainer. At about 10pm we drew in to what is known as Anzac Cove and were told to get ready to disembark. The din was by this time deafening and the whole peninsula from Anzac to Suvla Bay was fairly lit up with the flash of rifles and the bursting of shells and bombs. We were about a quarter of a mile from the shore, and every now and then we would catch a glimpse of a boatload of wounded men being conveyed to the numerous hospital ships moored about us. What has since been called the battle of Sari Bahr was then in full swing, and we knew that we were in for a hot time.

However, we all got ashore safely and received instructions to proceed to one of our outposts about a mile round the beach to the left. A deep sap led all the way along the beach to this outpost so we hopped into this and proceeded along. We were well under cover of the hills for a part of the distance, but the inferno of the previous night was still going on above us, and the bullets were whistling around in hundreds. One soon gets used to them but for a start you have an instinctive tendency to duck your head when they come very near. The sap had been blown in by Turkish shell fire in places and several of our men got hit while scrambling over. The Turkish snipers, who at this time seemed to be everywhere, watch such points and when a man shows himself they let him have two or three rounds before he knows where he is…

We were under the shelter of a small hill at this point and thought ourselves safe. The stray bullets from the Turkish trenches were coming right over the hill and falling right out in front of us. But our officers, who were as green as what we were regarding the "ways of war", had not counted on shrapnel or snipers, and we paid heavily for it. It was while we were having our dinner that the first big losses occurred. Some Turkish snipers who, judging from the direction the bullets seemed to be coming, must have been hidden somewhere on our left, opened rapid fire on us and men began to fall in all directions. To make matters worse the Turkish artillery opened fire on us and shrapnel was bursting over our heads. We were a splendid target for both snipers and guns, as we were all sitting in a heap when they first opened fire.

We were now ready to proceed to the firing line and set off just as it was getting dusk. Sari Bahr, where we were ordered to reinforce our chaps, was about a mile from where we then were and the route which we were to take led up through a deep valley. It was up this valley and up the ridges on either side that the New Zealanders had advanced on the previous Friday night. As I afterwards heard, they had met with very little opposition until actually on the very top of Sari Bahr and then—well, no doubt you have read of the desperate fighting that ensued.

We had advanced up this valley about half a mile, the Canterbury Company in advance, when the inevitable shrapnel began the burst over our heads again. The Turks had got the range beautifully this time, the shells bursting right over us every time… A regiment of Tommies, who were making their way down the valley, met us at this point and with everyone trying to get out of the way of the shrapnel at the same time an indescribable mix-up occurred. The Turks made their fire hotter than ever and I do not know to this day how I escaped being hit. Men were falling all around me, and the Tommies, who were all Irishmen, got fairly mad with excitement. How we finally extricated ourselves from the melee I do not know but we did it somehow…

The events of the next few days I have not a very clear recollection of, except that it was little else except blazing away at the Turkish trenches to keep them quiet. We all learnt what real hunger and thirst are like. The quart of water which we had in our water bottles when we left the beach was all most of us had for two days. We soon discovered that it was impossible to eat the bully beef when there was no water to be had, as the particular brand which the army allows us is like eating salt and, coupled with the great heat of the weather, it brings on such a raging thirst as has sent not a few men mad. So for the first few days it was nothing but biscuits. I remember that they frequently refused to go down, there being not enough moisture in my mouth to even damp them…

In case you may have heard different I may say that we never at any time held the whole of the great ridge known as Sari Bahr, but the most important part of it, known as Chunuk Bahr, was in our hands, and it was from our position here that, had we been able to hold it, we could have dominated practically the whole southern portion of the Peninsula. Much blame and ill feeling has been created between the Colonials and the Tommies over them not putting up a better fight when the Turks attacked, but I am inclined to think that, judging by the frightful losses sustained by the Wellington and Auckland Battalions while holding the position, we would not have done much better.

During these days our losses had been very heavy and a number of our men had been taken bad with dysentery and enteric fever. The smell of the bodies was becoming intolerable and the flies swarmed in millions. It was pitiful to see some of our wounded covered with them from head to foot but too weak to even attempt to chase them off. We were losing heavily every day, the numbers being sent away sick being quite equal to those killed and wounded.

After the first week things began to get a little better. The Turks saw that it was no use trying to further shift us from our positions and their fire, though still plenty solid enough, slackened off considerably. We began to get better food and more water, although that filthy water is still fresh to my mind and taste. Our allowance was now a bottleful per day (one quart). However, since our new daily rations of rice, bacon, and onions all had to be cooked by ourselves it did not leave enough water for our tea. Still it had to suffice. Although we had been told never to drink any of the water unless it had been boiled, we never had a chance to boil anything, except ourselves, during the first week and had to drink what little we got just as it was. The change from biscuits to bacon and rice was very welcome although being mostly amateur cooks we made a mess of things at the start…

After a fortnight in the trenches we were relieved and sent down to the beach for a spell, or at least so it was called. It proved to be no spell, however, for we were doing pick and shovel work of four hours on and four hours off night and day for a week… Our numbers had been so cut down by now that there were not enough men for the reserves, the result being that we had to do our twenty-four hours in the fringe line, eight hours in the supports, and sixteen hours pick and shovel. This made only eight hours sleep out of forty-eight and the condition of the men after a fortnight of this can well be imagined… Our company suffered heavily enough but not to the extent that the unfortunate Auckland and Wellington companies did. I think that those men of the Main Body, 2nd, 3rd, and 4th Reinforcements, who had stuck it right through deserved a Victoria Cross.

The Australians relieved us in the morning and we embarked aboard an Italian steamer the same night, reaching Lemnos Island in the early hours of next morning… We were about six weeks on the island altogether, and then were sent back to the Peninsula. The weather was now getting very cold and the day before I came away we had our first fall of snow followed by heavy rain. I was in the trenches that night and the water was over our boot tops in parts. It was bitterly cold in spite of the fact that each man had on warm clothes and overcoats. I had a pretty bad night of it and as I had been feeling crook with jaundice and a touch of enteric fever for several days, decided to see the doctor next morning. I accordingly went down to him and was ordered straight away to hospital, being put aboard the hospital ship (*Delta*) the same night…

You have of course read all about the evacuation of Anzac and Suvla Bay. The Australians and New Zealanders are now in Egypt I hear. It seems to have been a messed-up job from the start, but so far as those two positions are concerned I am certain that a further advance could only have been made at such a sacrifice that it would never have been worth it…

Cyril Molloy MC
Otago Infantry Battalion

20 June 1917
My Dear Mother,
Long 'ere this arrives you will have seen my name amongst the list of wounded. As soon as I got a chance I cabled you to let you know that it was nothing serious. I am tip-top now and am able to get out on the river and enjoy myself… When I was first hit I thought I had got it pretty badly—naturally I suppose. However, an examination proved I was all right. I got a bit of shrapnel in the shoulder and the wound is almost

healed now. I also got hit in the back of the head—the bit of shrapnel somehow dodged my steel hat. I got a small cut in my ear—all right now and the drum of my ear was perforated by the concussion of the shell, but is rapidly healing. When I look around and see some of the injured I begin to realise how lucky I was. It was a great day and I would not have missed the experience for anything.

We went "over the bags" at 3.10am, the big mines just going up on our left—a wonderful sight. The earth shook as great volumes of flames leapt from the earth… The chaps were over before the barrage started and kept well under it all the way. I was in command of the 4th Otago Company and our objective was the Hun front line and support trenches. We gained our objectives without a great deal of resistance, the Hun almost without exception surrendering everywhere. They came out of the dugouts with their hands up shouting "Kamerad." There was little fight left among them. We ran into a couple of machine guns here and there, which caused us a few casualties. However, we soon fixed them. Their machine gunners are good. They fire until they have no hope and then put their hands up. These fellows got no mercy.

Further on than our objective the Hun resisted more stren-uously, but our fellows swept on and gained every objective according to time and exactly as planned. The worst part of the business comes when the objective is gained and we have to dig in. However, we got to work in good style and, although the chaps were dog tired, kept them going until we were finished. This was the most anxious time as the Hun was going well by then and sending over a fair amount of stuff. My Company had a good deal of entrenching to do and we were just about completed when I got hit.

We got word that the Hun was massing for a counter-attack from a certain direction and Brigade wanted new trenches dug to meet the case. I was just plotting it out on a map and getting the exact location of the trench when I got landed. Fritz was going solidly at that time. The 4th Division of the Australians were going through us. He spotted them and put over a high explosive shrapnel barrage, of which we got the benefit. However, he did not have nearly the concentration of guns we had and his stuff was not nearly as deadly…

However, the whole thing was a great success, but I am afraid the casualties are not light. We seem to have had a fearful lot of officers' casualties in our battalion. In my Company four of us went out. One was killed, two wounded and as far as I know the other man is still going. Mother, we got off even more lightly than we expected. We have the Hun well beaten on land now, but they don't seem to know it—that is, the rank and file.

I was hit on the 7th of June in the afternoon and was in a hospital at Calais until the 15th when I came over here to Walton-on-Thames….The only wound they worry about here, and which is nearly right, is the one in the head. My ear is getting right also. Consequently I have been out boating on the Thames every day…

Cyril Molloy was wounded at Messines but recovered in time to be committed to the New Zealand Division's attack at Passchendaele four months later. He was killed there on 11 October 1917.

Leonard (Len) Mitchell Hart
Otago Infantry Battalion

October 19 1917
Dear Mother, Father and Connie,
In a postcard I sent you about a fortnight ago, I mentioned that we were on the eve of a great event, and that I had no time to write you a long letter. Well, that great event is over now, and by some strange act of fortune I have once again come through without a scratch. The great event mentioned consisted of a desperate attack by our Division against a ridge, strongly fortified and strongly held by the Germans, but the name of which I better not mention. For the first time in the brief history of our army the New Zealanders failed in their objective with the most appalling slaughter I have ever seen.

My Company went into action 180 strong and we came out thirty-two strong.

Still, we have nothing to be ashamed of as our commander afterwards told us that no troops in the world could possibly have taken the position, but this is small comfort when one remembers the hundreds of lives that have been lost and nothing gained. I will give you an account of the battle as near as I can without mentioning any names or exasperating the censor (should he happen to open this) too much.

On a certain Wednesday evening our Brigade received orders to proceed to the firing line and relieve a Brigade of Tommies who had two nights previously advanced their positions two thousand yards and had held the captured ground against several counter-attacks by the Huns. These Tommies had, however, failed to take their last objective and we knew before we left that we were going to be put over the top to try and take it.

At dusk we started off from the town where we had been billeted for a few days, in full fighting order, to proceed to the front line. Our track led over five miles of newly conquered ground without lines of communication, roads, or anything but shell holes half full of water. The weather had for some days been wet and cold and the mud was in places up to the knees. We struggled on through this sea of mud for some hours, and everyone was feeling pretty well done. It was quite common for a man to get stuck in the mud and have to get three or four to drag him out. You can have no idea of the utter desolation caused by modern shell fire.

The ground we were traversing had all been deluged with our shells before being taken from the Germans, and for those five miles leading to our front line trench there was nothing but utter desolation, not a blade of grass, or tree, here and there a heap of bricks marking where a village or farmhouse had once stood, numerous "tanks" stuck in the mud, and for the rest just one shell hole touching another… The ground was strewn with the corpses of numerous Huns and Tommies. Dead horses and mules lay everywhere, yet no attempt had been made to bury any of them.

Well, we at length arrived at our destination—the front line—and relieved the worn-out Tommies. They had not attempted to dig trenches but had simply held the line by occupying a long line of shell holes, two or three men to each shell hole… At 3 o'clock on the third morning we received orders to attack the ridge at half past five, which was just before daylight. We were accordingly arranged in three successive waves or lines; each wave about fifty yards ahead of the other. There was a certain amount of difficulty in this operation as it was pitch-dark and raining heavily.

When all was ready we were told to lay down and wait the order to charge. My Company was in the first wave of the attack which partly accounted for our heavy casualties. Our artillery barrage (curtain of fire) was to open out at twenty past five and play on the German positions on top of the ridge 150 yards ahead of us. It was to move forward fifty yards in every four minutes—that is to say we were to advance as our barrage advanced and keep 100 to 150 yards behind it.

At twenty past five to the second and with a roar that shook the ground, some three thousand of our guns opened out on the five-mile sector of the advance… Through some blunder our artillery barrage opened up about two hundred yards short of the specified range and thus opened right in the middle of us. It was a truly awful time—our own men getting cut to pieces in dozens by our own guns. Immediate disorganisation followed. I heard an officer shout an order to the men to retire a short distance and wait for our barrage to lift. Some, who heard the order, did so. Others, not knowing what to do under the circumstances, stayed where they were, while others advanced towards the German positions, only to be mown down by his deadly rifle and machine-gun fire.

At length our barrage lifted and we all once more formed up and made a rush for the ridge. What was our dismay upon reaching almost to the top of the ridge to find a long line of practically undamaged German concrete machine gun emplacements with barbed wire entanglements in front of them fully fifty yards deep. The wire had been cut in a few places by our artillery but only sufficient to allow a few men through it at a time. Even then what was left of us made an attempt to get through the wire and a few actually penetrated as far as his emplacements only to be shot down as fast as they appeared. Dozens got hung up in the wire and shot down before their surviving comrades' eyes.

It was now broad daylight and what was left of us realised that the day was lost. We accordingly lay down in shell holes or any cover we could get and waited. Any man who showed his head was immediately shot. They were marvellous shots those Huns. We had lost nearly eighty percent of our strength and gained about 300 yards of ground in the attempt. This 300 yards was useless to us for the Germans still held and dominated the ridge. We hung on all that day and night. There was no one to give us orders, all our officers of the battalion having been killed or wounded with the exception of three, and these were all Second Lieutenants who could not give a definite order without authority. All my Company officers were killed outright, one of them, a son of the Reverend Ryburn of Invercargill, was shot dead beside me.

The second day after this tragic business, we were surprised to see about half a dozen Huns suddenly appear waving a white flag. They proved to be Red Cross men and the flag was sign that they were asking for a truce to take in their wounded and bury their dead. It was granted and not a shot was fired on either side during the whole of that afternoon… Our stretcher bearers were able to go and take all our wounded from the barbed wire, a thing that would have been impossible other-wise… I went out and buried poor Ryburn. He came with the Main Body, but had not been in France long.

The proportion of killed to wounded was exceptionally high compared to other battles, owing to the perfect marks-manship of the German machine gunners and snipers. My Company has come out with no officers, only one Sergeant out of seven, one Corporal and thirty men. Even then we were not the worst off…

The results of our stunt you now know so no more needs

to be said about it except that we did as well or even better than some of the Divisions on our right and left. None of them took their objectives and I know for a fact that our Third Brigade's losses and those of the Australians were every bit as heavy as ours. The Second Brigade has at least the satisfaction of knowing that they held a few hundred yards of ground they took, and our commander has since told us that no troops in the world could possibly have taken the ridge under similar circumstances.

Some terrible blunder has been made. Someone is responsible for that barbed wire not having been broken up by our artillery. Someone is responsible for the opening of the barrage in the midst of us instead of 150 yards ahead of us. Someone else is responsible for those machine gun emplacements being left practically intact, but the papers will report another glorious success, and no one except those who actually took part in it will know any different…

Lieutenant General Godley glossed over the disaster on 12 October, describing the battle as "a very good day's work" that had gained the New Zealand Division 500 metres of ground and nearly 600 prisoners. The casualties from this attack and an earlier one on 4 October, he told Minister of Defence James Allen, were "not unduly heavy."

Cecil Bertram McClure MC
Otago Infantry Battalion

31 July 1918

Dear Mother and Father,

I have been in some queer places in my time, but never before have I been housed in a pigsty. That is where I am now, however, even with the trough out of which to feed… It has been a momentous week for me as well as for many another, as well as for the Company, which I commanded in the absence of the officer commanding, who was out in rest.

Division has been worrying and worrying the Fritzes opposed to us in such a way as to have him worrying what he was up against. In a captured diary we found the following: "Opposite us are the English, that is, the New Zealanders of the 42nd Division." They were well aware later who was troubling them…

As much to test the opposition as to gain better ground, we received orders to push and occupy certain trenches. Without a barrage, beyond a few Stokes mortars, we went to it. Bombers and Lewis gunners did the work and in fifteen minutes we had captured and consolidated trenches 500 yards in front and even pushed down the CTs [communication trenches] running into Fritz's lines. Only three prisoners were taken, but we accounted for over 100, captured six machine and two pineapple guns, and what must have been hard for Jerry, promptly turned these guns on him.

With his accustomed bravery he turned what artillery he had onto us and began pounding our positions, though with little effect. The next day, towards luncheon hour, he suddenly dropped a regular hailstorm of shells of all shapes and sizes, completely blowing in all the captured trenches and many of the bivvies. It was during this strafe that Division lost its ablest, most capable and most wonderful man—Dick Travis (VC)—a man devoid of fear, full of go, of pluck and with an initiative and cunning so far as the Huns were concerned that would have done justice to any Red Indian.

The strafe lasted over an hour and then the dirty Hun went on intermittently till about quarter to seven, when I think every shell that could fall, and fall without bumping each other, on the space allotted by Fritz and occupied by us, came down. For fifty minutes the storm lasted and then some of his stormtroops broke through our advance post and poured across country to our front lines. On the flanks our chaps simply played havoc with the attackers and none could get within striking distance. Down a deep sap in the centre, however, he overran one post and charged for our line.

I shall never forget the result of his mad action… No sooner did our support see what was doing than they up and went to it with the bayonet, and there ensued what might be called a race for our front line, while the posts in the line itself poured lead into the charging enemy. As suddenly, almost, as the contest began, it dwindled away. And as if on the instructional ground, the Huns came through our troops running on, but with hands well aloft and yelling beseechingly "Kamerad, kamerad."

…I promised my battalion at least fifty prisoners, but only twenty reached them. Intelligence says, "The others were killed by their own shell fire, which continued rather heavily on our support line." Our casualties during the attack itself were slight, but here again we lost one of our best officers and the knowledge of this, I'm afraid, was hardly conducive to the taking of many prisoners.

Brigade, Division, Corps and Army have all sent for reports of our successful repulse of the counter-attack, and the Army Commander has issued a special order of thanks to the New Zealand Division on its most successful work. All the bigwigs are pleased as punch about the whole show too, and so it is needless to say (that) our old tin hats fit us much better now than prior to the stunt.

Cecil McClure was a Divinity student at Knox Theological College in Dunedin when war broke out in 1914. He fought at Messines, Passchendaele, Ypres, and Rossignol Wood, twice winning the Military Cross. He should have won the Victoria Cross, but Major General Russell, the New Zealand commander, refused to nominate any of his officers for this award.

The Denniston, Jackson and Skinner letters have been reprinted by permission of the Hocken Library in Dunedin. The Molloy and McClure letters are from Letters From the Battlefield *and are reprinted by permission of the editor, Glyn Harper. Every effort was made to contact members of the Hart family for permission to reprint the two Len Hart letters but without success. We republish them here in the belief that they deserve to be seen by a wider public as an example of the courage and endurance of the New Zealand soldiers who fought at Gallipoli and on the Western Front in World War I.*

German prisoners bring in New Zealand wounded.

RSA Collection. Alexander Turnbull Library

A disabled tank blocks a New Zealand trench after an attack on the German lines.

RSA Collection. Alexander Turnbull Library.

Terrain like this faced the New Zealanders as they advanced under heavy machine gun and shellfire at Passchendaele and later Polderhoek Chateau.

RSA Collection. Alexander Turnbull Library.

Troops take water up to the front line at Rossignol Wood on the Western Front.

RSA Collection. Alexander Turnbull Library

New Zealand infantry dig in during the "100 days" advance that ended the war on the Western Front.

Alexander Turnbull Library

New Zealand troops wait to advance from front-line trenches.

RSA Collection, Alexander Turnbull Library

New Zealand gunners at work during a harsh winter on the Western Front.

RSA Collection. Alexander Turnbull Library

Troops attend the burial of a New Zealand officer.

RSA Collection. Alexander Turnbull Library.

Journey's End. The grave of Julian's battalion commander, Lieutenant Colonel George King, killed at Passchendaele on the morning of 12 October.

RSA Collection. Alexander Turnbull Library

Opposite page: For the fallen. A copy of the King's Scroll as sent to the families of New Zealand soldiers killed in the line of duty. This one honours 2nd Lieutenant Reginald Christophers, the last of four Invercargill brothers to die in World War I.

Christophers family archive

G v R 1

Dieu et mon Droit

HE whom this scroll commemorates
was numbered among those who,
at the call of King and Country, left all
that was dear to them, endured hardness,
faced danger, and finally passed out of
the sight of men by the path of duty
and self-sacrifice, giving up their own
lives that others might live in freedom.
Let those who come after see to it
that his name be not forgotten.

2/Lieut. Reginald Gillon Christophers
Otago Inf. Regt., N.Z.E.F.

EPILOGUE

THE SILENT DIVISION

From a young and virile people, predominantly agricultural,
highly intelligent, of unusually fine physique, a race of horsemen,
farmers, musterers, athletes and Rugby footballers, it was only
to be expected that its manhood, already subject to a system of
compulsory military training, should yield sterling material for the
purpose of war.[51]
    – Colonel H. Stewart, *The New Zealand Division 1916–1919*

The New Zealand Division, in which three of the Christophers brothers served, was formed in Egypt under Major General Sir Andrew Russell in early 1916. Composed of survivors of the Gallipoli campaign and reinforcements from New Zealand, it went to France to fight under his command in April that year.

Like Kitchener's new armies in Britain, the soldiers of the division were mostly volunteers and came from all levels of society—farmers, musterers, bushmen, labourers, miners and mechanics; office workers, teachers, lawyers and other professional men. Up to a quarter of them had been born in Britain or other parts of the empire, most were under 25, and over three-quarters of them had some form of military training or actual battle experience.

Over the next two-and-a-half years, the New Zealand Division would win itself a reputation as one of the finest fighting formations on the Western Front. At Armentières in early 1916, it held the line for four months until ordered south to take part in the Third Battle of the Somme. In this battle, it performed with distinction, capturing eight kilometres of the German front line, nearly 1000 German troops, and fighting its way forward for over three kilometres.

Nine months later came the division's brilliant, but again costly, capture of Messines. In March 1918 its stand before Amiens helped to close the gap between the Third and Fifth British armies on the Somme during the great

German offensive ("Kaiserschlacht") that could have won them the war.

In the Allied counteroffensive that began in August 1918 and finally ended the war on the Western Front, the New Zealanders were among the spearhead divisions, driving the Germans back in action after action. They ended hostilities in November with the capture of the French town of Le Quesnoy and at the forefront of the British advance.

The exception to this almost unbroken run of success was the Battle of Passchendaele where on 12 October 1917 the New Zealand Division lost over 2700 men killed, wounded and missing in a futile assault on German pillboxes and uncut wire—the worst single day in New Zealand's military history and its only real defeat.

In a foreword to the division's official history, Field Marshal Haig wrote that no division in France had built up a finer reputation, whether for gallantry in battle or for the excellence of its behaviour out of the line. According to Russell, the division's commander, Haig rated the New Zealand Division first-equal with the British Guards Division as a fighting formation. "Needless to say for nothing else."[58]

Under Russell's direction, the division would grow in skill and professionalism during its two-and-a-half years at the front. The "wave" attacks of the Somme battles that were so costly in soldier lives gave way to small-group "fire and movement" tactics based on sections and platoons. After the Somme, Russell drilled his men in these tactics before each major attack. In this way, the NZ Division took a full part in the tactical revolution that finally broke the deadlock on the Western Front.

The division that arrived on the front in April 1916 was structured around three infantry brigades and its support units of artillery, engineers, signals, ambulance and ordnance personnel. Supporting the combat troops was a matching administrative organisation in England. Its primary role was to receive reinforcement drafts from New Zealand, train them and send them on to France. It also provided hospital and convalescent care for the wounded and managed their return, after retraining, to the front.

Most troops arriving in France from mid-1916 went first to the Bullring at Etaples for further combat training, but the New Zealanders did most of their training at Sling Camp in England. Here they bayoneted straw-filled dummies, jumped down trenches, threw Mills bombs and learned to fire rifle grenades and light machine guns.

Their day-to-day experiences, however, were typical of those of all British and dominion soldiers on the Western Front. Except for major offensives, they were in action for no more than a few days a year. The rest of the time was spent in bringing food, water and munitions up to the front line, building or repairing trenches, burying telephone cables, and keeping wire entanglements in good order. Battalions did a four to eight day tour of duty in the trenches then went back to their billets in the rear for a "rest". Within hours they would be drilling, training, or toiling in endless working parties. "In summer, trench life could be tolerated; in winter it was pure misery."[59]

The New Zealanders were arguably better disciplined than the two other colonial formations, the Canadians and the Australians. There were just over 2000 courts-martial for the 100,444 New Zealanders who served overseas in the NZEF, compared to 23,000 courts-martial for the 331,814 Australians who served overseas in the AIF; 18,000 courts-martial for the 458,218 Canadians who served with the CEF. In short, the percentage of New Zealand courts-martial to troops in theatre was less than one-third of the Australian rate and half that of the Canadians.

On other counts, the New Zealanders did not rate so well, wrote Steven Loveridge. Among these were the widespread use of foul language, bingeing on alcohol, and rates of VD infection estimated to be the highest among the soldiers of the empire.[60] Along with these traits went a general inability to achieve a "polished finish in saluting," generally regarded as a hallmark of military discipline. It was an attitude they shared with other colonial troops who believed it was servile to salute a man who had not earned respect by personality or performance in the field.

There were also serious breaches of the rules of war. New Zealand troops killed wounded and surrendering Germans in their attack on enemy trenches during the Third Battle of the Somme, and in a number of other reported cases. Infantryman Norman Gray wrote: "Perhaps you have never reflected on the shooting of Germans who hold up their hands and yell 'Kamerade.' It may seem an atrocious thing to shoot or bayonet such a man, but when you remember that up to the very moment of shooting up his hands, he has been sitting behind his machine gun pouring death into the advancing line, you cannot wonder that there is little quarter given. There are very few men in a charge who can control themselves under such circumstances."[61]

Significantly, the war gave the men of the New Zealand Division a new sense of themselves, an appreciation of the qualities that were marking the soldiers of Britain's dominions out from those of the home country—"physical prowess, mental toughness, a laconic yet humorous spirit, egalitarianism, ingenuity."[62] The journey to self-awareness began in Egypt and continued at Gallipoli where the New Zealanders experienced in full the chronic inefficiency and unearned privileges of the British officer class. The British troops, against whom they had often been measured, appeared puny and lacking in initiative.

"Our men are taller and stronger, deeper chested, better muscled, more resolute in attack, stronger in defence," wrote Ormond Burton with conviction based on observation. "Their general standard of intelligence was much higher. Besides them the English looked like adolescent boys."[63]

About colonial soldiers in general, Russell had similar views. "No doubt the overseas troops are better fighters than the Home article," he wrote to his son Andy. "This is not because they are better men really for we all come of the same stock, but because we are better fed, and in the case of men, as of sheep, half the breeding goes down the throat." As for the British Territorial troops at Gallipoli, Russell found them not only difficult to motivate but lacking in physique and fighting spirit.[64]

Initially, the New Zealanders had formed a poor impression of the Australians, based on the larrikinism and poor discipline they had witnessed in Egypt. The Gallipoli and Western Front campaigns were to change all that, as the New Zealanders developed an ongoing admiration for the fighting skills of their colonial brothers.

Social reform campaigner Ettie Rout, however, saw some clear differences between the two: "The New Zealanders are islanders; the Australians continentals. Quiet steadfastness characterises the first, reckless daring the second… The New Zealanders tend to respect authority, or at least not to offer needless affront to it, and they rely on precedent: the Australians rely on their own individual judgement and the Great God Chance. The restraint of his feelings is as natural to the New Zealander as the frank and ready expression of them is to the Australian. On the march the New Zealanders never sang: the Australians scarcely stopped singing."[65]

As did the British regiments, which sang constantly on the march. A poignant memory for men who fought on the Somme was a Welsh battalion "moving up in the dark, their voices rising in that most beautiful of hymns, *Aberystwyth,* until the voices were lost in the sound of shellfire." Or a badly mauled Welsh Guards battalion singing in a wood behind the village of Gouzeaucourt, "In the sweet bye and bye we shall meet on that beautiful shore." By contrast, New Zealand troops generally came across to outsiders as "stern, dour and grim." An English observer was moved to dub them "The Silent Division".

In spite of its exemplary performance, the contribution of the New Zealand Division to final victory on the Western Front was necessarily small. At Gallipoli the New Zealanders were a significant part of the Allied campaign to force Turkey out of the war. Now they found themselves "but a tiny element in a vast Allied effort along an endless front." There was much less opportunity to stand out, wrote military historian Ian McGibbon, "not only because of the numbers involved but also due to the nature of the fighting."[66]

Few troops in the Allied armies, however, would surpass the New Zealanders as fighting soldiers. On the Western Front they gained a reputation for reliability, sense of purpose and determination, courage, steadiness and discipline, wrote McGibbon.[67] In a letter to Minister of Defence Allen in March 1918, Godley enclosed a list of the battle honours so far won by the New Zealand Division on the Western Front, commenting: "There is no doubt that honours have been given to it (the division) more freely, and in a larger proportion to its numbers, than to any such force or unit of the British Empire employed in this war."[68]

Pugsley concluded: "At Messines in 1917, at Passchendaele in victory on 4 October and defeat on 12 October, and in the battles of 1918, the New Zealand Division proved itself a superb, professional fighting machine, despite its amateur status." By 1918, he wrote, the division was qualitatively superior to any other division on the Western Front.[69]

The division, however, paid a high price for its proficiency and battlefield success. Some 12,500 of its soldiers were killed during its time on the Western Front—the highest rate of loss in the whole of the British Empire, according to historian John Terraine. Many more would die in the following years from the effects of wounds, disease or general ill health.

Shell shock, or what came to be more accurately known as Post-Traumatic Stress Syndrome, damaged many others, some permanently. In most cases the cause was not concussion from shellfire but combat fatigue or exhaustion, caused by too many days in the front line, lack of sleep, exposure to the elements, and the ever-present threat of death from gas, shellfire or bullet.

Veteran Ormond Burton wrote: "No man can take it forever. Keep tension on strongly enough and long enough and almost every man in time will deteriorate. The signs were often very clear—a man would drink more heavily. Smoking was the surer indication. A cigarette to steady the nerves, then two, then three, then the chain effect. All the time the nicotine that apparently soothed was steadily undermining the nervous system until another brave man had to toss it in and go back."

The grimness of war on the Western Front, however, had its compensations, among them a strong sense of community and some of the closest friendships these men, if they survived, would ever know. For this reason, infantryman Norman Hassell almost regretted the end of hostilities in 1918, and believed that most of his mates in the division did also. No more, he wrote, would a man know his friends in times of danger, knowing that they would willingly give up their lives for his, and that he would do so for them. The true glory of war, wrote another New Zealand soldier, was to be found not in battle—"a thing of horror and wanton waste"—but in courage, comradeship, self-sacrifice and service.[70]

ACKNOWLEDGEMENTS

As always in the writing of history there are people who help to make it happen. In particular, I want to thank the Christophers family—John, Herb, Paul and James—who provided essential material from their archives and photographs from their collections. Lynley Dear, archivist at Southland Boys' High School Museum, published a fine but fictional account of the Christophers brothers' story in 2010 and inspired me to go one further. Alison Clarke from the Hocken Library in Dunedin and Marilyn Domney from the Wellington City Library gave me timely help in accessing the soldiers' letters published here, and my very special partner, Barb Freeman, donated her technical and proofreading skills. My special thanks also to Jenny Haworth of Wily Publications Ltd for taking a chance on this book in a difficult publishing environment.

ENDNOTES

INTRODUCTION
1 Ormond Burton. *The Silent Division.* p. 121
2 Christopher Pugsley. *Gallipoli: The New Zealand Story.* p. 358
3 Ibid. p. 360

1. IN THE BEGINNING
4 Erik Olssen. *Murihiku. The Southland Story.* Ed. Paul Sorrell. p. 72
5 G.A. Hamilton. *History of Northern Southland.* p. 98
6 From Christophers family archives
7 From Christophers family archives

2. VICTOR JAMES ("VIC")
8 Ian McGibbon. *The Path to Gallipoli: Defending New Zealand 1840–1915.* p. 122
9 Steven Loveridge. *Calls to Arms: New Zealand Society and Commitment to the Great War.* p. 105
10 Sergt C.G. Nicol. *The Story of Two Campaigns.*
11 Steven Loveridge. *Calls to Arms.* p. 103
12 Terry Kinloch. *Echoes of Gallipoli: In the Words of New Zealand's Mounted Riflemen.* pp. 31–35
13 Godley to Minister of Defence James Allen, 25/3/1915
14 Paul Fussell. *The Great War and Modern Memory.* p. 106
15 Major Fred Waite. *The New Zealanders at Gallipoli.*
16 From Christophers family archives
17 From Christophers family archives

3. HERBERT HENRY ("HERB")
18 Paul Fussell. *The Great War and Modern Memory.* p. 91
19 Nicholas Boyack and Jane Tolerton. *In the Shadow of War.* p. 57

4. JULIAN ANTHONY
20 Minister of Defence James Allen to Godley, 7/8/1917
21 Jock Phillips, Nicholas Boyack, E.P. Malone. *The Great Adventure.* p. 104

5. REGINALD GILLON ("REG")
22 From Christophers family archives
23 Richard Holmes. *Tommy.* p. 72

7. GROOMED FOR WAR
24 Allan Davidson, "New Zealand Churches and Death in the First World War" in *New Zealand's Great War.* Eds John Crawford and Ian McGibbon. p. 454
25 Jock Phillips. *A Man's Country? The Image of the Pakeha Male – A History.* p. 156
26 Steven Loveridge. *Calls to Arms.* p. 25
27 Allan Davidson. p. 450
28 Ibid. p. 450
29 Ibid. p. 454
30 Peter Lineham. "First World War Religion", in *New Zealand's Great War.* Eds John Crawford and Ian McGibbon. p. 478
31 Steven Loveridge. *Calls to Arms.* p. 211
32 Ibid. p. 50

33   Ian F. Grant. *Newspapers During the First World War.* p. 130
34   Steven Loveridge. *Calls to Arms.* p. 39
35   Barbara Tuchman. *August 1914.*

8.   THE REASON WHY
36   Glyn Harper. *Letters From the Battlefield.* p. 154
37   Steven Loveridge. *Calls to Arms.* p. 26.
38   Ian McGibbon: "The 'kith and kin' factor was a strong influence behind the majority support of
     the population for the country's continuing involvement in World War I. Most New Zealanders
     had been in the country for 40 years or less, and only in the 1890s had the numbers of locally
     born New Zealanders outstripped those born in the British Isles. Ties to the 'Old Country' were
     strong and most New Zealanders were proud to be part of the British Empire." From a public
     lecture titled "The Shaping of New Zealand's War Effort – August to October 1914".
39   Barbara Tuchman, in Steven Loveridge, *Calls to Arms.* p. 206.

9.   COUNTING THE COST
40   Christopher Pugsley. *Gallipoli. The New Zealand Story.* p. 358
41   Ibid. p. 353
42   Glyn Harper. *Letters From the Battlefield.* p. 13
43   Stevan Eldred-Grigg. *The Great Wrong War.* p. 260
44   Ibid. p. 260
45   Damien Fenton. *New Zealand and the First World War: 1914–1919.* p. 41
46   Stevan Eldred-Grigg. *The Great Wrong War: New Zealand Society in WWI.* p. 183
47   Ibid. p. 327
48   Phillips, Boyack, Malone (Eds). *The Great Adventure.* p. 231
49   Damien Fenton. *New Zealand and the First World War.* p. 49
50   Steven Loveridge. *Calls to Arms.* pp. 192, 199, 203

10.   THE PITY OF WAR
51   John Terraine. *To Win a War: 1918, the Year of Victory.* p. 192
52   Ormond Burton. *The Silent Division.*
53   Richard Holmes. *Tommy.* p. 531
54   Phillips, Boyack, Malone (Eds). *The Great Adventure.* Introduction
55   Christopher Pugsley. *Gallipoli. The New Zealand Story,* p. 356
56   Glyn Harper (Ed). *Letters From the Battlefield.* p. 14
57   Stevan Eldred-Grigg. *The Great Wrong War.* p. 296

EPILOGUE: THE SILENT DIVISION
58   Col. H. Stewart. *The New Zealand Division 1916–1919.* p. 191
59   Jock Vennell. *The Forgotten General.* p. 297
60   Martin Middlebrook. *The Kaiser's Battle.*
61   Phillips, Boyack, Malone (Eds). *The Great Adventure.* p. 103
62   Steven Loveridge. *Calls to Arms.* p. 101
63   Ibid. p. 134
64   Jock Vennell. *The Forgotten General.* p. 90
65   *Quick March.* Royal New Zealand Returned and Services Association. 10/3/21
66   Ian McGibbon. *New Zealand's Western Front Campaign.* p. 359
67   Ibid. p. 358
68   Godley to Minister of Defence James Allen, 1/3/1918
69   Christopher Pugsley. *On the Fringe of Hell.* p. 300. McGibbon is less fulsome: "In reality, all
     the (ten) dominion divisions were good, New Zealand's included, and there were probably a
     dozen British divisions that were equally impressive. During the last year of the war, it (the New
     Zealand Division) was one of the better divisions on the Western Front. Not only its size and
     proficiency but also its ample reinforcements made it a formidable force."
70   Ian McGibbon. *New Zealand's Western Front Campaign.* p. 358

BIBLIOGRAPHY

PUBLISHED SOURCES

BOYACK, Nicholas. *Behind the Lines: The lives of New Zealand soldiers in the First World War*. Allen and Unwin/Port Nicholson Press. 1989

BURTON. O.E. *The Silent Division. New Zealanders at the Front 1914-19*. Angus & Robertson. 1935

BURTON, O.E. *The Auckland Regiment NZEF, 1914–1918*. Whitcombe and Tombs. 1922

BYRNE, Lt A.E. *Official History of the Otago Regiment NZEF in the Great War 1914–1918*. J. Wilkie and Co. 1921.

CARLYON, Les. *Gallipoli*. Pan Macmillan Australia. 2001

DUNN, Capt J.C. *The War the Infantry Knew 1914–1919*. Jane's Publishing. 1987

ELDRED-GRIGG, Stevan. *The Great Wrong War: New Zealand society in World War I*. Random House. 2010

FENTON, Damien. *New Zealand and the First World War: 1914–1919*. Penguin. 2013

FUSSELL, Paul. *The Great War and Modern Memory*. Oxford University Press. 1975

GILBERT, Martin. *The First World War*. Weidenfeld and Nicolson. 1994

HARPER, Glyn. *Massacre at Passchendaele: The New Zealand story*. HarperCollins Publishers. 2000

HAMILTON, General Sir Ian. *Gallipoli Diary*. Edward Arnold. 1920

HAMILTON, G.A. *A History of Northern Southland*. The Southland Times Company Ltd. 1952

HOLMES, Richard. *Tommy: The British soldier on the Western front 1914–1918*. Marshall Pickering. 2004.

HASTINGS, Max. *Catastrophe: Europe Goes to War 1914*. William Collins. 2013

JAMES, Robert Rhodes. *Gallipoli*. B.T. Batsford. 1965

KEEGAN, John. *The First World War*. Hutchinson. 1998

LAFFIN, John. *Damn the Dardanelles:The story of Gallipoli*. Doubleday. 1980

LAFFIN, John. *British Butchers and Bunglers of World War I*. MacMillan Australia. 1989

LEED, Eric J. *No Man's Land: Combat and Identity in World War I*. Cambridge University Press. 1979

LOVERIDGE, Steven (Ed). *New Zealand Society at War 1914–18*. Victoria University Press. 2016

MacDONALD, Lyn. *They Called It Passchendaele*. Michael Joseph. 1978

McGIBBON, Ian. *The Path to Gallipoli: Defending New Zealand 1840-1915*. GP Books. 1991

McGIBBON, Ian. *New Zealand's Western Front Campaign*. David Bateman. 2016

MacKAY, Don (Ed.). *The Troopers' Tale: The history of the Otago Mounted Rifles*. Turnbull Ross Publishing. 2012

NEILLANDS, Robin. *The Great War Generals on the Western Front 1914–1918*. Robinson. 1999

NICOL, Sergt C.G. *The Story of Two Campaigns: Official war history of the Auckland Mounted Rifles Regiment 1914–1919*. Wilson and Horton.. 1921

NORTH, John. *Gallipoli: The Fading Vision*. Faber and Faber. 1936

PHILLIPS, Jock. *A Man's Country?The Image of the Pakeha Male: A History*. Penguin Books.1987

POWLES, Col. C.G. *The History of the Canterbury Mounted Rifles 1914–1919*. Whitcombe and Tombs. 1928

PUGSLEY, Christopher. *Gallipoli: The New Zealand Story*. Hodder and Stoughton. 1984

PUGSLEY, Christopher. *On The Fringe of Hell: New Zealanders and Military Discipline in the First World War*. Hodder and Stoughton. 1991

SORRELL, Paul (Ed.). *Murihiku: The Southland Story*. Southland to 2006 Book Project/Dan Davin Literary Foundation. 2006

STEWART, Col. H. *The New Zealand Division 1916–1919: A popular history based on official records Vol. 2, France*. Whitcombe and Tombs. 1921

TOLERTON, Jane. *An Awfully Big Adventure*. Penguin Group. 2013

TRAVERS, Tim. *The Killing Ground: The British Army, the Western Front and the Emergence of Modern Warfare, 1900–1918*. Allen & Unwin. 1987

TRAVERS, Tim. *Gallipoli 1915*. Tempus Publishing. 2001

WAITE, Major Fred. *The New Zealanders At Gallipoli*. Whitcombe and Tombs. 1919

WILKIE, Major A.H. *Official War History of the Wellington Mounted Rifles Regiment, 1914–1919*. Whitcome and Tombs.

UNPUBLISHED SOURCES

Malone, Col. W.G. MS Papers. Alexander Turnbull Library

Correspondence: General Sir Alexander Godley, Hon Sir James Allen (1912–1915) WA 252/1. Archives New Zealand

Correspondence: General Sir Alexander Godley, Hon Sir James Allen (1915–1918). WA 252/1. Archives New Zealand

Correspondence: Hon Sir James Allen, General Sir William Birdwood, Major General Russell (1914–1920). WA series. Archives New Zealand

War Diary: HQ NZ Mounted Rifles Brigade. WA 40/1. Archives New Zealand

War Diary: New Zealand & Australia Division. WA 20/2. Archives New Zealand

Reports on Operations, New Zealand & Australia Division. WA 10/4. Archives New Zealand

NZEF Operation Orders, Gallipoli. Col W.G. Braithwaite. WA series. Archives New Zealand

Sari Bair Operation File. WA 20/5. Archives New Zealand

Routine Orders, Brigadier General A.H. Russell, Commanding No.4 Section. WA series. Archives New Zealand

Operations Reports: New Zealand Division (1918). WA 20/3 (8). Archives New Zealand

ARTICLES

DAVIDSON, Alan. "New Zealand Churches and Death in the First World War." In *New Zealand's Great War*. Eds John Crawford and Ian McGibbon. Exisle Publishing. 2007

GRANT, Ian F. "Newspapers During the First World War". Ibid.

OPENHEIM, Roger. "The Impact of the Great War on NZ Education". Ibid.

McGIBBON, Ian. "The Shaping of New Zealand's War Effort, August–October 1914".